THE
COMPLETE GUIDE TO

FASHION
ILLUSTRATION

THE
COMPLETE GUIDE TO

FASHION
ILLUSTRATION

COLIN BARNES

NORTH
LIGHT
BOOKS

Cincinnati, Ohio

To my mentor Elizabeth Suter, my models, and all
aspiring fashion illustrators.

© Macdonald & Co Ltd 1988

First Published in Great Britain in
1988
by Macdonald & Co (Publishers) Ltd
London & Sydney

A member of Maxwell Pergamon Publishing
Corporation plc

First Published in North America
in 1988 by North Light Books, an
imprint of
F & W Publications, Inc.,
1507 Dana Avenue,
Cincinnati, Ohio 45207.

ISBN 0-89134-250-8

Filmset by Tradespools Ltd, Frome, Somerset

Printed and bound in Italy by O.F.S.A. Milan

Research and development: Mary Lee Woolf

Historical Introduction: Elizabeth Suter

General Editor: Frances Kennett

Senior Editor: Judith More
Senior Art Editor: Clive Hayball
Designer: Andrew Smith
Picture Researcher: Veneta Bullen

CONTENTS

INTRODUCTION

*'Costume is the
mirror of history'
Louis XIV*

Fashions, and fashion
illustrations, reflect a great
deal of the style and
attitudes of their era. It is
worth studying the work of
great illustrators from the
past to understand the
many different ways in
which they conveyed the
clothes and the mood of
their time.

Colin Barnes: Gouache

A HISTORICAL PERSPECTIVE

Above: 'The Swing' – Kangra painting (circa 1815). In this allegorical Indian miniature there is an immaculate blend of colour, line, pattern and poetic mood.

Below right: 'Thalea preparing for her wedding' – Greek vase (5th century B.C.). This disarmingly simple drawing gives a very precise description of the fine linen tunics, hair styles and jewellery worn by Etruscan women.

Far right: Detail of a boar and bear hunt – Flemish tapestry (15th century). The medium of woven tapestry was another way in which craftsmen were able to record descriptions of the styles and fabrics worn by men and women of all classes.

From the moment man made marks on cave walls – followed by the temple frescoes and bas-reliefs of Egypt, the Hellenic sculptures, the cultures of the Orient and on to the paintings of Western civilizations – we have inherited a vast and accurate knowledge of the clothes worn by men and women, and an unquenchable interest in fashion.

Throughout the centuries artists must surely have been inspired by the telling behaviour and colour of fabric. Great use was made of drapery and the costumes of their subjects to emphasize the drama of their work. This is apparent in the religious and secular paintings, the sculptures and carvings, tapestries and mosaics of the Middle Ages.

THE ARRIVAL OF PRINT

The sixteenth century symbolized an explosion of learning and exploration; a unique period of development and high artistic creativity and invention, with the opening up of trade routes throughout Europe and the known world. A forerunner to this new age of communication, and vital to its advance, was the introduction of the printing press in the middle of the previous century by Johannes Gutenberg. With the powerful patronage of the nobility and heads of state, artists were encouraged to move from court to court, exchanging ideas and extending their knowledge. We must be grateful to those who left records made for their own use when working

Woodblock by Donzella di Brabantia (1598). From the pioneer book of costume *Habiti Antichi et Mondo di tutto il Mondo,* depicting contemporary styles.

Engraving by Richard Gaywood after Wenceslaus Hollar (1654), the first to illustrate fashion as a means of artistic expression.

on a painting, freely drawn but detailed studies of figures and their costume, anticipating the fashion illustrator of the future. Although still a long way from the first recognised fashion plate, it was around this time that we begin to see the issue of portfolios of engravings and books compiled by artists, and concerned solely with national dress and contemporary fashion. But despite the increase in the number of plates depicting the mode of the day for both men and women which circulated the wealthy European capitals, these must be regarded as chronicles of current social customs in dress styles, rather than illustrations of fashion; since the purpose of the illustrator is not merely to comment but also to project the design of the garment.

THE FIRST TRUE FASHION ILLUSTRATIONS

Halfway through the seventeenth century we glimpse the first positive interest in fashion illustration in the etchings of Wenceslaus Hollar, working in London from 1640, and despite the constraints of his medium, producing the most delicate, natural and descriptive drawings of garments and texture. Until the latter part of the century the spread of information was confined to engravings and fashion dolls, complete in every detail and scaled down to about a third of the human body. However, with the arrival of *Le Mecure Galant* in 1672, a newspaper which included articles that dealt solely with fashion, and founded through the support of the lavish court of the powerful Louis XIV (which had become the predominant influence on the cultural, economic and social life of Western Europe), the widespread dissemination of ideas began.

From the eighteenth century onwards fashion ideas began to flow through newspapers and magazines, mainly from France and Italy, reaching out to Scandinavia and beyond to Russia in the East, and across the Atlantic to the new lands of North America. Yet in these early days periodicals were essentially the prerogative of the élite. Prints, made from wood engraved blocks, always informative and charming, were becoming less stilted, attributable to the skill of the engraver and increased refinement of the copper engraving. Many artists were skilled in these techniques and made their own plates; but often in order to keep up with demand these imported plates would be tampered with and re-engraved, receiving small additions and emphases to the styles and not infrequently weakening the spirit of the original work. Often depicted were groups of men and women together, making a historical statement not only about clothes but about the furnishings of a fashionable house, or indeed its external appearance. At this point we notice fashion plates dealing specifically with certain articles of dress and accessories, and the manner in which they might be worn: men and women's elaborate and often bizarre hair styles, men's hats, caps and shoes. Always the figures were placed in context, which might be a shadow or strip of ground; but more generally the illustrator would use the rectangular shape of the copper-plate to frame and enhance his drawing by posing the subjects against an appropriate background.

THE RISE AND FALL OF THE FASHION PLATE

It was not until the second half of the eighteenth century, during the reign of George III, that the pioneer English periodical *The Lady's Magazine* was launched in 1759, and is reputed to have reproduced the first engraved fashion plates in answer to public demand. However, in France, with the impetus imparted by Louis XIV, fashion was becoming an organised industry of great economic importance. It has continued in prominence until today despite the devastation of the French Revolution, and the depletion of dressmakers and tailors, many of whom fled to England never to return. Notable among them were Marie Antoinette's Minister of Fashion, Mlle Bertin, and Niklaus von Heideloff, a miniaturist who settled in London. His folio, *Gallery of Fashion*, made its debut in 1794 and contained finely executed hand coloured aquatints of English fashions – for English ladies! Expensive to produce and published by subscription, its readership was necessarily limited. Eventually von Heideloff was sponsored by Rudolf Ackerman, himself a refugee, whose journal *The Repository of The Arts* contained many engraved plates of great quality and charm, often accompanied by a risqué text. For a short time German publishers, taking advantage of the collapse of France, became the dominant source of fashion news throughout Europe, circulating the brilliant and witty engravings of Daniel Chadowiecki and later Ernst Ludwig Riepenhuisen.

Aquatint published in the *Gallery of Fashion* – Niklaus von Heideloff (1797). It depicts early eighteenth century fashionable walking dress.

French engraving from a series entitled *'Le Bon Genre'* (1810). This one is of English Empire walking out attire.

11

Above: Engraved fashion plate published in *Le Petit Courier des Dames* (1837). An accomplished and delightful indication of the figure-moulding corset worn by fashionable ladies of the time.

Opposite: Line drawing of swimming costumes by Charles Dana Gibson (1900), the creator of the prototype 'Gibson Girl'.

In France itself the publisher Pierre la Mesangère commissioned sets of engravings from Philip Louis Debacourt and Horace Vernet. Not only did these delightful works provide fashion information but they also made a commentary on social custom. The redistribution of wealth and power, along with the ascent of the professional and middle classes stemming from the destruction of the profligate court of Louis XVI and Marie Antoinette, left their mark on the whole of Europe and signalled a natural break point between the eighteenth and nineteenth centuries.

Across the Channel, Britain too was entering a period of immense social and technical change; built on the foundations of the Industrial Revolution laid in the previous century. Technical improvements in printing, the invention of photography, and the appearance of the sewing machine heralded a progression of communication on styles of dress. Fashion features appeared in newspapers and periodicals to keep pace with the demands of an affluent society concerned with fashion as an outward expression of its philosophy. Caricaturists of the period enjoyed exaggerating the more extreme fashions, such as the wide-brimmed, flower- and feather-trimmed hats, but it was *Godey's Lady's Book*, published in 1830, which first introduced a serious approach to fashion to the general public.

During the last decade of the eighteenth century Napoleon Bonaparte, fearing a decline in the prosperity of France, encouraged the regeneration of the textile industry, which adopted manufacturing methods invented and already in use in England. By so doing he attracted dressmakers and tailors and all the other essential elements of the industry to the capital, and by the 1850s had established Paris once again as the supreme force in fashion. The ruthless demand for information from Paris led to a lowering of standards and the quality of fashion engravings began to suffer. The informative outpourings from the French studios, with the bright exception of Jules David, were over-worked and lacked graphic vitality. In this century the gold framed Victorian fashion print was much admired, and often seen regaling the walls of lesser fashion establishments. While some of the work produced in the second half of the nineteenth century has charm, for the most part it is mechanical and repetitive, and does not compare well with the artistic distinction of illustrators before and after this period.

THE TWENTIETH CENTURY: A NEW APPROACH

The twentieth century began with hope and a spirit for change as befits a new age. A reaction against early nineteenth century Romanticism in the preceding years had created different attitudes. In England, William Morris, founder of the Arts and Crafts Movement with his concept of craftmanship and requirements for decoration, and Arthur Lasenby Liberty, with his refreshing insistence on the Pre-Raphaelites' reform style of dress for women and exotic purchases from the Far East for his shop in Regent Street, had helped to clear away the clutter of high Victorian sentiment. The ornamental style of Art Nouveau, which touched European architects, designers and illustrators alike and directed them towards symbolism, must be linked with Morris and his followers. Two graphic exponents of Art Nouveau were Alphonse Mucha and Aubrey Beardsley, with his powerful use of black and white and artificial imagery.

The momentous arrival in Paris of Diaghilev's *Ballet Russe*, with Léon

13

Above: Illustration by Pierre Brissaud for *La Gazette du Bon Ton* (1914). The strong shadow cast by the tree's foliage heightens the dramatic effect of the drawing and accents the whiteness of the Jeanne Lanvin dress. The tree was a very successful device often used by Brissaud.

Right: Illustration by Georges Lepape for *La Gazette du Bon Ton* (1912). Lepape's work reflects all the excitement of the new age. Paul Poiret's innovatory designs are complemented by Lepape's spectacularly colourful stylisation of the interior of a theatre.

Bakst's fabulous designs and drawings, was to prove a most significant influence upon the life style of the new age. In 1908 Paul Poiret, the daring French couturier and disciple of the new artistic mood, brought out a small exclusive edition of his own innovative designs, illustrated in an appropriately vivacious and colourful manner by Paul Iribe, and followed in 1911 by a similar edition illustrated by Georges Lepape. This appears to be a pointer, for in 1912 the adventurous publisher Lucien Vogel, in collaboration with Michel de Brunhoff, a future editor of French Vogue, launched *La Gazette du Bon Ton* – a journal of exceptional quality and the forerunner of all fashion magazines as we know them today. Among the

Robes pour l'été 1920.

group of artists employed to illustrate *Bon Ton* were A. E. Marty, Georges Barbier, Charles Martin, J. and P. Brissaud, Paul Iribe, Georges Lepape, and later Eduardo Benito, Umberto Brunelleschi, Pierre Morgue and Étienne Drian, whose expressive figurative drawings were quite unlike the stylised drawings of his contemporaries. It is interesting to compare their attenuated figures and flat application of colour and pattern with the graphic simplicity of the Japanese woodcut of the eighteenth century.

The World War of 1914–18 marked one of the greatest social upheavals in History, and the ensuing effect on the arts and applied arts was equally dramatic. Avenues of exploration begun before 1914 – the work of Braque, Picasso, Matisse, Modigliani, and the sculptures of Brancusi, the birth of Cubism and later Fauvism and Dadaism – found their explosive conclusions after the war. The fabric of society, particularly the arts, underwent an extraordinary change. The war ensured that women no longer remained objects of adornment, and from their emancipation there emerged Coco Chanel, arguably the greatest fashion stylist of the twentieth century.

The dynamic force of Cubism, Art Deco and the new image of women was reflected in the drawings of *La Gazette du Bon Ton*, which ceased independent publication in 1925. It was acquired along with other Vogel enterprises by the charismatic Condé Nast who had been publishing American *Vogue* since 1893, and later introduced French *Vogue*. He continued to use the European contributing artists to swell the ranks of the established American *Vogue* illustrators, among whom were George

Litho print by Raoul Dufy for *La Gazette du Bon Ton* (1920). This delicate print shows fabrics by Bianchini.

Litho drawing by Jean Dupas for *Fourres Max* (1928/9). This impressive drawing, highlighted in silver, appeared in the de luxe fashion album *Toi*.

Above: *L'homme Elegant* by Eduardo Benito (1920). A formal, monochrome composition, superbly drawn and controlled. Such skill led to Benito's splendidly uncompromising and powerful work for *Vogue* in the thirties.

Right: Magritte fashion design. An unexpected facet of the Surrealist painter René Magritte, the work shows all the simplicity and strength of design to be found in his paintings.

Plank, Helen Dryden and Douglas Pollard. From time to time painters were commissioned to illustrate fashion, notably Raoul Dufy, Magritte, Jean Dupas, Marie Laurencin, Kees van Dongen, and Robert and Sonia Delaunay. At the height of Surrealism Salvador Dali and de Chirico were prominent. Cecil Beaton, ultimately regarded as a photographer and stage designer, contributed light-weight and witty sketches for *Vogue* in the thirties. Felix Topolski and Ruskin Spear also made their social comments, along with the tentative observations on the English scene by John Ward. More recently the work of Andy Warhol, David Hockney and Richard Hamilton was commissioned, underlining the relationship of fashion illustration to art movements.

THE GOLDEN YEARS

The three decades which led up to 1939 can be regarded as the golden years of fashion illustration. Credit for this must go to the patronage of the exclusive magazines, which nurtured their artists and gave them seemingly limitless freedom and opportunity. Over and over again reference has to be made to a handful of leading journals from the three capitals, since theirs was a declared policy of commitment to the drawn and painted image, as yet unchallenged by the camera. Advertisers too were dependent on the drawing to display their wares, often using the artists employed on the editorial pages.

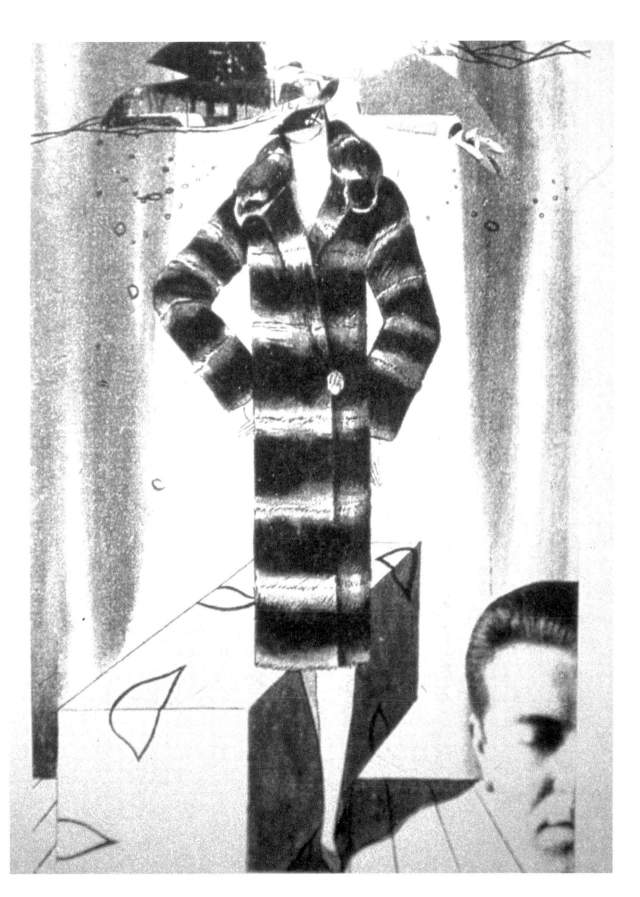

In time we begin to see a clear divergence between editorial work and the needs and demands of the advertisers. *Vogue* and *Harper's Bazaar* had been joined by others – *Femina*, *Journal des Dames et des Modes*, *Modes et Manières d'Aujourd'hui* and in Germany *Die Dame*. *Harpers* had Erté under contract, but it is to the Condé Nast organisation that we should pay tribute for its visionary leadership.

The confident French artists of the Jazz Age dominated the magazines with their witty and lucid style. Elongation of the body, economy of line and boldness of design was their hallmark. The covers of *Harper's Bazaar* and *Vogue* were illustrated by Erté, Lepape and Benito; the latter's cubistic treatment deserves special attention. The artists of the three supreme decades of fashion drawing exhibited a masterly control of their craft, the result of disciplined and extensive study; many had received a formal training at the *Ecole des Beaux Arts*.

Recession in the economies of the USA and Europe led to further major social changes. The emancipation of women's fashion of the twenties gave way to a new romanticism. There emerged a brilliant draughtsman Carl Erikson, known as Eric, whose expressionist handling of loose brush work in line and colour wash was in direct contrast to techniques then current, and would change fashion graphics for the next twenty years. It is interesting to note that Benito, master of the twenties stylization, much admired the Erikson approach and adopted it with varying success.

Shortly afterwards René Bouet-Willaumez (RBW), a Frenchman and artist of comparable strength, joined *Vogue* magazine as one of their principal illustrators, along with Jean Pagès and Pierre Morgue. Christian Bérard, with a background of fine art and theatre, having initially worked for Harpers Bazaar moved across to Vogue and made important contributions veering towards a surrealist image. Drawings by René Gruau began to appear before 1939, but his voluptuous and powerfully graphic designs, reminiscent of Toulouse-Lautrec and Mucha, only reached maturity after 1945. Though extensively used editorially, he is one of the first artists to be identified with advertising, mainly for Christian Dior. His work is still frequently to be seen, and is a remaining link with the age of the fashion illustrator superstars.

Above: Erté (Romain de Tirtoff) cover for English *Harpers' Bazaar* (1933). By his authoritative use of red, black and white in this forceful design, Erté has achieved a stunning effect to which every cover artist should aspire.

Left: Jacques Demachy designs featured in *Femina* magazine (1932). Three attenuated figures silhouetted against a window emphasise the fashionable cool, dark colours of the clothes.

Above: Vertès for English *Harpers'
Bazaar* (1937). An economical use of
line and colour. The girl's tactless
and hollow gesture is meant to
startle.

Right: Francis Marshall
advertisement for Jaeger (1938).
Already, Marshall's bold and
polished style was attracting
advertisers.

Far right: Eric (Carl Erikson) for
American *Vogue* (1941). Evening
dresses, available from Bergdorf
Goodman, seen at a war-time
benevolent dance. This
characteristic drawing shows Eric's
influential and distinctive work.

JAEGER
for Christmas

JAEGER HOUSE, 204, REGENT STREET, LONDON, W.1.

THE ADVENT OF FASHION PHOTOGRAPHY

With hindsight, we can see that towards the end of the thirties the work of
some excellent photographers, among them Steichen, Horst, Hoynigen-
Huene, Beaton and Man Ray, signalled the decline of editorial fashion
illustration. The Second World War engulfed civilization and caused
further enormous social and economic repercussions. Fashion reflected
the austerity of the times and most Parisian journals ceased publication;
leading artists escaped to New York and continued to work from there.
War conditions prevailed, and there was no significant fashion statement
until 1947 when Christian Dior launched the New Look.

Magazines returned gradually to normal publication and illustrators
shared honours with photographers, already beginning to emerge as the

Far left: René Gruau for *Album de la Mode du Figaro* (1946). Evening co-ordinates by Pierre Balmain. By this time, Gruau was getting into his stride and producing sensational work.

Left: RBW (René de Bouet-Willaumez) for American *Vogue* (1941). A cocktail suit at Bergdorf Goodman. RBW worked in the Expressionist style set by Eric, but in his own refined manner.

premier force. René Bouché, who had begun to work in 1941 from New York now joined Eric, RBW, Bérard, Bernard Blossac, Gruau, Demachy and Tom Keogh, a superbly colourful American artist. Also working at this time was Francis Marshall, who had produced sensitive drawings before the war, and had developed a very strong, commercial black brush line which reproduced well in newsprint and made him popular with advertisers. Frequently, however, the constraints of advertising denied the freedom of expression coveted by artists. Although the New Look provided inspiration for superb drawings, the death of Eric in 1958 and Bouché five years later marked the end of illustration as a major means of communication in the glossy magazines.

Above: Caroline Smith, popular editorial artist of the sixties who makes full use of the rectangular, flat pattern and tonal values reminiscent of the twenties.

Right: Antonio (Antonio Lopez). An internationally recognised illustrator with an eclectic approach to style, and a powerful influence on contemporaries.

The sixties began a new fashion phenomenon: youth culture erupted on an unprecedented scale. In London Mary Quant and Barbara Hulanicki of Biba spearheaded a new era of inexpensive boutique fashion aimed at limitless new markets. At this time the superficial, decorative drawings of wide-eyed doll-like figures typified the current youthful fashion. But two illustrators, Eric Stemp and Angela Landels, continued to draw in the tradition of artists trained in the life class. In the United States John Fairchild produced the informative and professional trade newspaper *Women's Wear Daily*. His string of artists included Kenneth Paul Block, Stipleman, Pedro Barrios, Perleman and Stephen Melendez. Trade journals were to prove a continuing source of work for illustrators, not of the same glamorous indulgence as the pre-war magazine editorials, but more immediate and informative. Whilst the tradition of the graphic editorial had been broken with the death of Bouché, one artist alone, Antonio Lopez, appeared to keep alive the role of the star illustrator. Although working frequently on an international basis, he was not used by magazines with the same continuity as his predecessors.

FASHION ILLUSTRATION TODAY

Sonia Delaunay: In the first half of the twentieth century, revolutionary art forms strongly influenced fashion. Brilliant colours and striking new silhouettes challenged the established conventions regarding dress and body shapes, while an interest in all things ethnic inspired bold 'barbaric' jewellery.

In the last few years illustrators have returned to favour as the creators of exciting images for ideas or products. Perhaps people have grown too accustomed to the definition and brilliance of photography; perhaps advances in video technique have helped to encourage a new market, one quite willing to see pictures in fractured, highly coloured, very stylised and often witty graphic forms.

In the presentation of fashion, however, the supremacy of photography is unlikely to be overtaken. Advertisers, editors and promotion companies will always use camera and film as the prime medium for illustrating fashion, as they have done for the past thirty years. But the role of the photographer is more likely to be challenged now than at any time during these past three decades.

Fashion illustration may never return to the heights of acceptance that it enjoyed between 1920 and 1940, because the causes of its popularity and excellence are no longer to be found. Style is conveyed nowadays in a multitude of ways, through many more magazines, through day-long television output, by an international popular music industry and a vast and diversified consumer marketplace. The illustrators of the pre-war years worked in miniature by comparison, for a small audience, when creating and communicating 'a look'.

For the first fifty years of this century, a significant influence on the fashion world came from the various revolutionary art movements. The brilliant colours of the Fauves found their way into printed fabrics; Cubism prompted strange new silhouettes, experiments with dress and body shapes to mirror the new perceptions of form in paint. All the new art movements inspired some new direction in fashion: Expressionism, a fresh appreciation of colour and mood; Futurism, the use of industrial materials for fashion; Dadaism, in some equally irreverent fashionable objects, and Surrealism, in fabrics (Schiaparelli had its leading exponents – Dali, Magritte and Ernst – design her dress fabrics). One most influential event was the arrival of Diaghilev's *Ballet Russe* in Paris, in 1909 (see page 13). The pre-war world was closely linked with other emerging art forms too. Breton and Man Ray photographed couture in Paris; Picasso and Braque were influenced by the art of Africa, rediscovered in the late thirties, and in turn this appeared in the new 'barbaric' jewellery made of early plastics and glass by Chanel's jewellery designer, Comte Etienne de Beaumont.

By the end of World War II this sensitive link between the world of fine arts and fashion had become tenuous. Couture fashion in Paris reached a peak of influence and was depicted in both line and photograph, for a time, side by side. But new influence on European mass culture, American film and the coming of television, created other images of beauty and style. By the end of the fifties fashion was becoming more democratic, and the newer art forms – pop music, film, photography – exercised greater influence on designers than painting. A late exception was Op Art, the last direct expression of an art movement in high fashion. Its geometric shapes, stripes and dots form the basis for many eye-dazzling fabrics, and design and colour themes from this movement found direct expression in youthful clothes, particularly in the work of Quant and Courreges in the early sixties.

Blossac: Here realism is controlled within the overall vigorous design.

LEARNING SKILLS

The general decline in drawing skills is not only due to changes in artistic influence on fashion. There has been a major shift in emphasis in art education. British Art education was founded in the nineteenth century and generally fine art courses provided an academic training which incorporated a range of studies covering traditional drawing techniques, the study of architecture, and other specialist crafts, such as work in wood, stone or clay.

Since the 1950s the emphasis has moved into other areas. The influence of the Bauhaus movement in Germany, believing that technical improvement, even factory methods, could lead to new ways of producing objects of great beauty, was very strong, and opposed to the 'art for art's sake' school of thought. American Abstract Art also led to a reaction against academic training in favour of self-expression, and craft became a dirty word. During the 1950s a number of less academic commercial art courses became available. The social and cultural changes of the sixties gave birth to a generation expressing themselves through abstract rather than figurative means. The study and practice of fine art ceased to be regarded as providing the right background for fashion illustrators.

Christopher Brown (above): Hand-crafted knitwear with strong visual impact here illustrates the keynotes of seventies style, the youthful exuberance and vitality of which were clearly reflected in fashion illustration.

Colin Barnes (right): This illustration epitomises the eighties emphasis on a more positive fashion image for men – adventurous in line, colour and materials.

By the 1970s, artistic values had altered again. Less optimism and greater austerity was reflected in visual arts and music. Rebellion seemed not so worthwhile, and artistic expression returned to figuration, to a directly emotional, hand-crafted way of working. The style was rough and ready at times – echoing the exuberance of punk music in the late seventies. The emphasis was not on acquiring skills, but on creating an instant impact, a strong message. As in every decade, illustration changed in keeping with the mood expressed in the other visual arts.

The cultural movement has changed again in the 1980s. The most significant shift has been towards a 'minimalist' presentation which is particularly evident in fashion design. However, in comparison with previous decades the eighties have seen more transitory trends than ever before. At the same time, the seventies tendency to overlook technical skills in favour of self-expression is still prevalent, leaving many present-day students feeling frustrated. They no longer have the skills or technique to put down on paper what they want to express, when diversity is increasing. Today students are asking for anatomy lessons. Neither extreme, rigidity or indiscipline, is right.

It can be difficult for the aspiring illustrator to decide what type of formal art education can provide the best grounding for a career in fashion illustration. Currently in Britain there are no courses which offer a comprehensive training for the would-be fashion illustrator. In America the situation is better. Fashion illustration often falls between two stools – as a poor relative in the fine art school, or as a useful minor tool of trade for the clothing designer. Illustration teachers often have to take classes in rooms full of sewing machines instead of drawing facilities; live models are hardly ever considered essential.

The best line of approach is to find a good course on illustration geared towards fine art, in preference to a course on fashion design where the emphasis is on creating clothes, not learning how to draw. In this way the student at least builds up a strong, formal background that will enable him or her to progress in their working life. To survive as a fashion illustrator you must have the technical skill to change direction some-times, to find new modes of expression and, above all, to work with discipline as an artist.

DRAWING

Line drawing is a graphic, strong way of expressing the essential elements of clothing and figure, in a simplified fashion. The artist builds on this, perhaps allowing for areas of colour to be used in a dramatic way. The true essence of line is exemplified by Matisse – significantly, an artist who represented the human form with truth, clarity and memorable beauty.

Colin Barnes: Gouache

THE EXPRESSIVE USE OF LINE

Matisse (above): Nude. An extremely simplified drawing that nevertheless has complete conviction. The anatomy of a back and arm lifted and slightly twisted is so familiar that the line gives perfect expression to it.

Degas (right): Ballerina. An apparently simple drawing, yet the artist conveys a sense of a body in motion, balanced on one leg. Although the skirt obscures the torso, the line of the body is perfectly followed through and the shape of the figure is perceived easily.

'Line' can mean two things in the world of fashion. In design, the 'line' of a dress refers to the overall statement of the shape – not merely the outline silhouette, but the tendency of the new direction. The season's 'line' can be emphatic and square, or soft and rounded. It might be allied to geometric textiles, in an angular look, or to draped fabrics for an elongated effect.

The fashion illustrator has to develop the ability to make a 'line drawing', which is a bold, graphic version of the designer's intention. The work must be expressive, not merely accurate and representational. Most commissions will be to illustrate one figure and most probably not in any context. Possibly there will be a group of figures, so that composition may come into the task. But the essential function of the line drawing is to tell the story of dress, and convey the mood of it. The background should never overwhelm the figure but play second place to it, and provide a subtle adornment.

The best way to become successful at line drawing is to study drawing from life. That enables you to create a convincing human figure to clothe with the designer's new ideas. As in all artistic fields, only once you know the rules well is it possible to play with them, distorting the body for interesting effects. When the drawing of the body is confident, the artist is freed to imbue it with emotion.

This comes naturally to some extent; one artist may draw with energy, or another may prefer to draw with delicacy. Many people do not flourish learning life drawing, preferring a totally graphic approach that leads them to make very strong images of figures in a flat pattern concept. But the general rule is that the more technique and skill acquired, the more details become available for achieving a desired effect. For example, an artist wants to make a strong, athletic figure in sporty attire. Sound knowledge of the back muscles, how they dip in and curve at the base of the spine, can help – the drawing uses that detail with a flourish, instantly conveying the message.

Drawing from life needs to be done with supervision, but there are ways to develop awareness independent of it. Studying the past can be enriching. Look at the stylized drawings of the early Egyptians, the apparent simplicity of a Matisse figure, or the restrained lines of a

Degas

Japanese woodcut. There are no superfluous lines or details. Decide for yourself what makes these drawings successful, to build your awareness of the possibilities.

The pose of the model conveys mood and atmosphere. Sometimes it is revealing to adopt the pose yourself, to mirror the image, and imagine the mood. Is it graceful, aggressive, haughty, energetic, sensuous, or innocent? When you begin life drawing it will be challenging enough to get the shape right at first, but an awareness of this other quality in a pose does no harm.

It can help to start drawing the human figure by mapping out the structure of the body using simple vertical and horizontal lines. Visualise the ground plan and use it as a guide to relate the proportions of the body to the pose. Delineate the head as an oval form; if the head tilts to one side consider the diagonal line of the axis. If the neck twists round, the drawn line should indicate this movement. Continue the drawing by describing each form as a series of lines and spheres. Notice the triangle formed from the nipples, navel and horizontal lines of the shoulders. Once the basic structure has been sketched out, use a variety of line to refine forms until their tension begins to be like those of the model.

Try drawing the model in different positions and record how the outline changes as you move around the figure. Vary the length of time spent on recording each pose. If the model is standing, look carefully to observe where the weight of the body is centred. If the model is standing on the left leg, the visual force and stretch of the movement will create tension on the left side, while the right will seem more relaxed. The shoulder of the left side will be lower than the right, and the left hip will be tilted to one side, and project outwards. In essence, you are working towards a representation of a human form that is convincing. Incidently, remember that in real life nothing has a drawn line around it and that your drawn lines need not define the edge of an object.

Drawn lines are two-dimensional marks. Experiment with the effects and illusions you can create by varying the proportion of lines, the angles of inclination, the placing and spacing of lines, and by using different materials. For example, a simple follow-up on class work could be to re-draw poses you have studied in a number of different textures, pencil, charcoal, ink and so on.

THE MOVING FIGURE EXERCISE

Capturing the movement in a pose ensures that the vitality of that moment survives. The key to portraying movement is to show where the strain comes, and in real life this strain inevitably creates muscle tension. This exercise helps you to see how the body's shape changes as it moves, transferring weight from one foot to the other. It also reveals the importance of a clean line, and teaches the discipline of drawing upwards rather than downwards. Depending on where the student is sitting, he or she may find figures walking towards them and overlapping, in which case it is necessary to use a different colour for each pose – not only for clarity, but because the cleanness of line lends overall coherence.

Take a large sheet of paper. Using a coloured marker or crayon, draw the figure in outline, using a continuous, clean line. As the model assumes a new pose she takes only one step forward, moving on alternate feet. Therefore for each pose the position of one foot is in common with the previous one. Always draw each new pose with a different colour, beginning at the foot which fits the previous drawing. Draw upwards towards the head. When the drawing is finished, check the proportions.

Repeating the moving figure
exercise (see page 35) will help
to achieve accurate outline
drawings of figures in motion.
Having completed the drawing,
the image can be built up by
adding detail and tone.

Colin Barnes: Series of figures drawn rapidly in movement.

THE SINGLE LINE EXERCISE

Students of life drawing tend at first to see a feathery, hesitant line and work on too small a scale, barely occupying the white space of the paper. Try this exercise, which will help to develop concentration, and produce bolder, more confident lines on the page.

Stage One (far left)
Take a large sheet of paper and define the form of the model's body without taking your pencil off the paper at any point. You can go back over a previous line, and you can pause, but never lift the pencil or you will break concentration and lose the flow.

Stage Two (left)
Still keeping your pencil on the paper, simplify your bold outline with flat colour to create a clear, graphic image.

The studio sketch right demonstrates how important a sure line is to a fashion illustrator. Work on Stages One and Two to develop the ability to produce a quick, effective rough from a live model. Eventually you will be able to take your pencil off the paper at times and still produce a flowing, confident image.

41

DRAWING FROM A PHOTOGRAPH

Some illustrators may find it easier, ultimately, to compose a picture using photographs, but a knowledge of anatomy is essential in the first instance. One of the problems is that photographs are only two-dimensional, and to make a successful drawing, a three-dimensional aspect of an object is needed in order to make a convincing representation of it. Beginners are often seduced by photographs into a misguided concern with unimportant superficialities, such as shading, or copying tricky poses. This is of little use in a profession where a primary skill may well be to draw a lifelike pose from a model running along a catwalk in a few minutes. However, photographs are invaluable references for details, accessories, or architectural backgrounds.

Colin Barnes: This set of drawings exemplifies the practising of figure drawing without a model. Choose photographs from magazines that show a figure in movement – preferably a catwalk shot, where the weight is thrown to one side causing the hip to jut out. This will help you to produce a drawing that is lively, and has some personality of its own, instead of a static copy.

43

Mats: Pastel. A strongly conceived
illustration that uses both a bold
cut-off view of the body, and a full-
frame shape, reminiscent of
photography but imbued with
another style because of the freely
coloured technique. But remember
that illustrators do not always have
control over the framing or the page
area that their work will occupy.

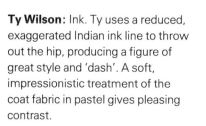

Ty Wilson: Ink. Ty uses a reduced, exaggerated Indian ink line to throw out the hip, producing a figure of great style and 'dash'. A soft, impressionistic treatment of the coat fabric in pastel gives pleasing contrast.

45

EXAGGERATION AND ABSTRACTION

Once you can draw a figure accurately, you will understand and appreciate better the quality of exaggerated details or simplified abstractions. Good abstract drawings are not the result of inexperience. Anyone who takes the view that a four-year-old could produce a Matisse, Picasso or Bridget Riley, is misled. Certainly they may be able to copy it, or produce naive visuals which appear abstract in form, but they will lack the experience and conceptualising that lies behind even the simplest abstract. Exaggerations and distortions in great artists' work are the result of vast exploration, and made in a knowledgeable and 'calculated' way to give expression to their feelings.

For example, an artist may wish to distort the proportions of the body by elongating the legs, or stretch the neck to suggest grace and elegance. Enlarging the shoulders or torso gives an impression of strength, while minimising the waist or exaggerating the roundness of the hips and bottom creates flattering shapes for clothes.

The ultimate result of such distortions can be to produce a drawing where the form of the body is so reduced that it states the current fashion 'line' in a powerful, entirely abstract way. Whether you aim for an entirely realistic depiction or a virtual caricature of a model, the 'accuracy' of such drawing is really only judged by the power of the final illustration.

Composing an image concerns how you put the figure on the page: how you crop it, use it whole, or place it in a group. Background is only an enhancement to that. Occasionally an artist is required to produce a full scale illustration for a top-class magazine or publication. Such commissions are not really fashion illustration but more to do with creating a fashionable picture to boost the image of the publication itself. The fashion illustrator spends a small amount of time on 'composition', in comparison with the work of figure drawing alone.

Natasha Ledwidge: Ink. This drawing demonstrates the power of dramatic line. The circular shapes, exaggerated with an almost caricatured, cartoon-like energy, capture the style and humour of the puffball skirt craze.

Lawrence Mynott (right): Collage. A full-length figure that uses exaggeration to convey style. The elongated legs emphasise the shortness of the skirt, while the bold black hat balances out the composition.

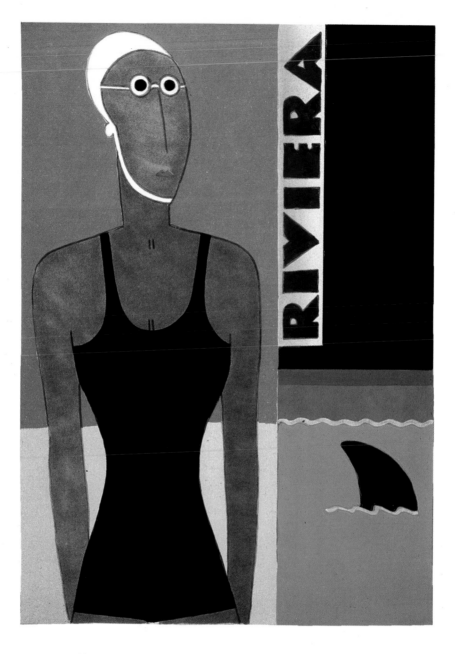

Michael Roberts (above):
Gouache. A black swimsuit on the
Riviera is given a humorous
treatment with a period feeling in
keeping with the subject – the
Mediterranean is associated with
'modern artists', and the swimmer
looks suitably intense and modern
herself.

Phan van My (right): Gouache.
Matisse is hinted at in another
composition of three figures, but
here the emphasis is on glamour;
merely suggesting the texture,
colours and fabrics of the men's
clothes.

FACES

and

MAKE - UP

The essence of good illustration of the face is to create an almost abstract stylishness, at once personal and fashionable. Every detail has to be communicated: the hair-style, the make-up, and accessories must be accurate. However, first and foremost the overall impression should be one of attraction.

Colin Barnes: Gouache

DRAWING FACES

Another very important part of the figure, the face, provides a focal point and must be rendered in harmony with the character of the body and the mood of the clothes. A badly drawn face will ruin an otherwise good illustration. Faces, hands, and feet are the most difficult features to draw, and the solution is not to ignore them but to practise constantly drawing them. Lighting and styling will play an important role in rendering faces and accessories, and much can be learnt by setting up your own compositions to try out new and imaginative styles of portrayal.

Colin Barnes (below): Pastel. This drawing makes an editorial point visually; varied eye colours and eyeliners are fashionable. The light technique suggests an experimental attitude to new colours.

Phan Van My (right): Acrylic and pastel. This illustration suggests the collage work of Picasso. It is an original and ambitious way to make the point visually that make-up can succeed in creating flattering transformations.

MY

EXERCISE IN DRAWING THE HEAD

It is important to understand the basic shape of the head, and its components. Students are often afraid of the head, thinking it more complicated than it really is to draw.

Stage One

Regard the head as an inverted egg (below; trace round it the three lines, or planes of the face, on which the eyes, nose and mouth are positioned. Now twist the head, tilt it up and then down, and experiment with the shaping of the curved lines where the mouth, nose and eyes will be.

Notice that when the head is tilted down, a large flat plane for the top of the head becomes visible, and the space between the lines for the eyes, nose, mouth and chin, will be closer together. Correspondingly, when the head is thrown back, a line representing the jaw will have to be curved upwards, and the planes of the features will be closer together towards the top of the inverted egg.

Stage Two

The changing shapes come clear with constant repetition. Once mastered, the placing of colour for emphasis will be easier to do. In the second drawing (right), colour was applied in a loose, decorative way, to roughly follow the contours of the face and the direction of the plane-lines.

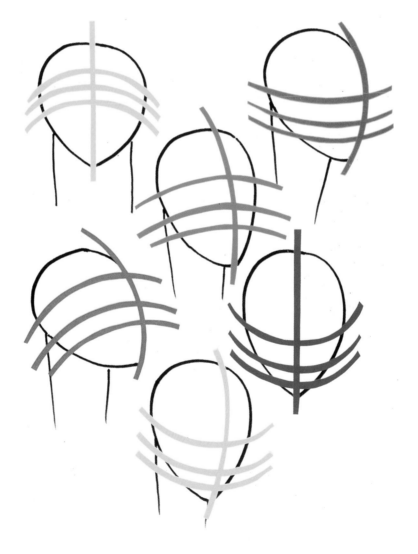

Sharon Long (left): Collage. A witty illustration for a bra feature gives vitality and character to a conventional subject, using brown paper collage and charcoal.

Ty Wilson (right): Ink. A minimal line drawing in Indian ink makes a strong statement about new silhouettes in hair fashion.

Colin Barnes (below): Collage. This was made for a feature on hair accessories; the hairstyle was discussed with the beauty editor beforehand. Styling is often planned for beauty features in this way, not left to the artist's discretion.

Colin Barnes (left): This strong pastel was created for a beauty feature in *Cosmopolitan* magazine.

Hazel Gomes (above): Watercolour. This illustration was executed when the artist was designing jewellery for Yves Saint Laurent. Being an illustrator as well as a designer enabled Hazel to present her ideas not only for accurate information, but most decoratively too. Not one detail of the jewellery is obscured, the creation of mood and style being conveyed by the facial expression, treatment of the skin, and the opulent, suggestive drapery of the turban.

Hazel Gomes: A bold illustration
that depends on a confident reading
of the head shape; the planes of the
faces are understood well enough
for a minimal presentation of them.
The angles of the hand, the chin,
and the hat itself are accurate, and
make a balanced composition.

Ty Wilson (above): Acrylic and line. This shoe illustration is strong enough to be considerably reduced in size and still have impact.

Colin Barnes (above): Collage. These sunglasses demonstrate the need for tight, crisp technique when an illustration will be reproduced in a small area on a magazine page, and fight with text and other visual material, possibly photography, for effect.

Hazel Gomes (below left): Acrylic. Sometimes an artist is given a very specific layout to illustrate, where the type may fit round a picture and space for the illustration is marked out precisely. Hazel's handbag is an example of this sort of work.

COLOUR

PATTERN

and

TEXTURE

Be aware of tonal strength, and colour balance, but above all, use colour purely. The fashion illustrator must be able to create images of crispness and clarity. Think big, be happy, and use big brushes and large pots of colour at first, to overcome timidity.

Colin Barnes: Pastel

USING COLOUR

Colour theory is fascinating, and in recent years has been extended by the more technical or scientific explanations promulgated by advertisers and manufacturers, to help understanding of the colours that can seduce, attract, or satisfy the customer. The art student can find many good books specifically on this subject to broaden their appreciation of how colour affects us. But quite frankly from the point of view of the fashion illustrator, colour theory is not of great significance. Use of colour is more of an emotive issue. The illustrator has to simulate the actual colour of the object, and apart from suggesting a complementary skin tone, and maybe a small amount of background colour, it is unlikely that there will be a chance to explore further – except very occasionally for a prestigious magazine, where lavish backgrounds are called for, and colour balance then becomes an important consideration.

It is important to use colours purely and not let them get muddy and flat. You can mix colours deliberately with black or white, to see the effect, before going on to mix together different colours. The most interesting effects are only assimilated by trial and error, not by learning rules from books. Sometimes, when working in watercolour, beautiful colours emerge by chance, just on the rim of the plate or palette, and you find happy combinations you can repeat.

If colouring proves difficult, work with gouache, and apply it thickly to eliminate the white of paper. Use the colours as if you are designing a poster that must attract attention at a distance. Or some collage work, to appreciate the effect of flat areas of colour, will often help.

Think how instinctively and vigorously children use colour, and fill spaces. Enjoy colour: use a big wide brush (a two-inch size), dip it into a

Werner (left): In this bold expressionist image bright colours are used in blocks to suggest a mood, an emotion, and a strong tactile sense. The composition gives the illustration great impact, with the form bursting out of the frame of the area.

Maurice Arrari (overleaf): To suggest the characteristic fluidity of silk, try representing the movement or disruption in a printed fabric pattern. The body in motion is a particular feature of this artist's work.

Tricosa Collection in

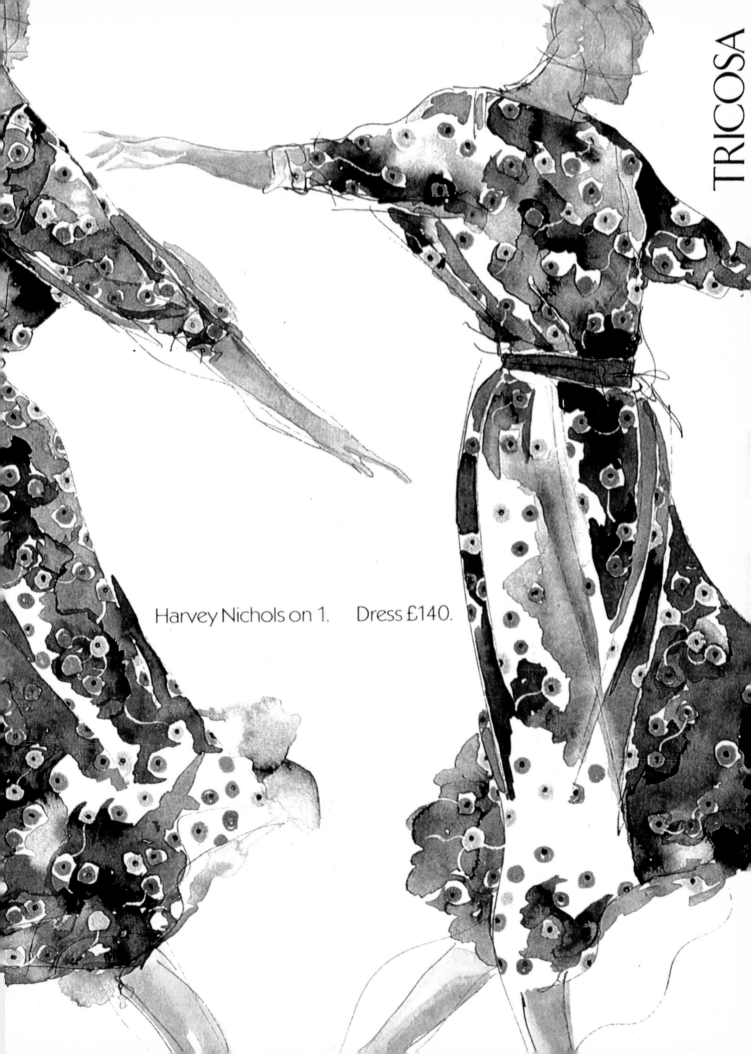

TRICOSA

Harvey Nichols on 1.   Dress £140.

Arie (above): A limited palette here used to good effect with a skilled choice of accent colours, bold lines and curves.

Michael Roberts (right): A treatment of colour that relies on a seemingly simple, yet sharply defined, geometric composition for its effect.

pot of bold colour, gouache or poster paint, and working on a positively inviting large sheet of paper, splash on a great quantity to fill a simple outline that you have created. Do not worry about perfect shapes, neat little outlines. Limit yourself to three primaries at first, and repeat the exercise with pastels, white mixed into all the colours, and one highlight.

Do not feel inhibited about copying the greatest colourists – Matisse, Rothko, for example, or the charcoal and pastels of Toulouse Lautrec. Look at paintings to see how a mood has been evoked by the colouring, then try to achieve it yourself. It is always relevant to examine other work, so long as it produces your own fresh, individual response.

Phan van My (left): Delicately balanced pastel tones in a Matisse-like collage. The mirrored image of the model, framed by the rectangle helps to centre attention on the figure. This type of illustration would be used decoratively alongside a beauty care feature.

Sharon Long (above): Compare this check jacket with that on page 74; meticulous rendering is only one way to convey the character of a fabric. Here the play of colour where the woven threads cross is imaginatively suggested with tissue paper collage.

71

Stavrinos: A pencil drawing that invokes our perceptions of monochrome film and photographic images to suggest glossy surfaces. The close-up of one small section of the garment worn by the figure at top right, clearly shows how the illustrator has used varying density of tone to achieve the desired impression.

Mats: A soft, light surface in pastel actually suggests the bulk of fur more than its hairiness, but the imagination is fired. Again, the close-up detail brings the method under the magnifying glass. See how he uses close-set, elongated dots to build up the 'fur' rather in the manner of the Impressionist's pointillist technique.

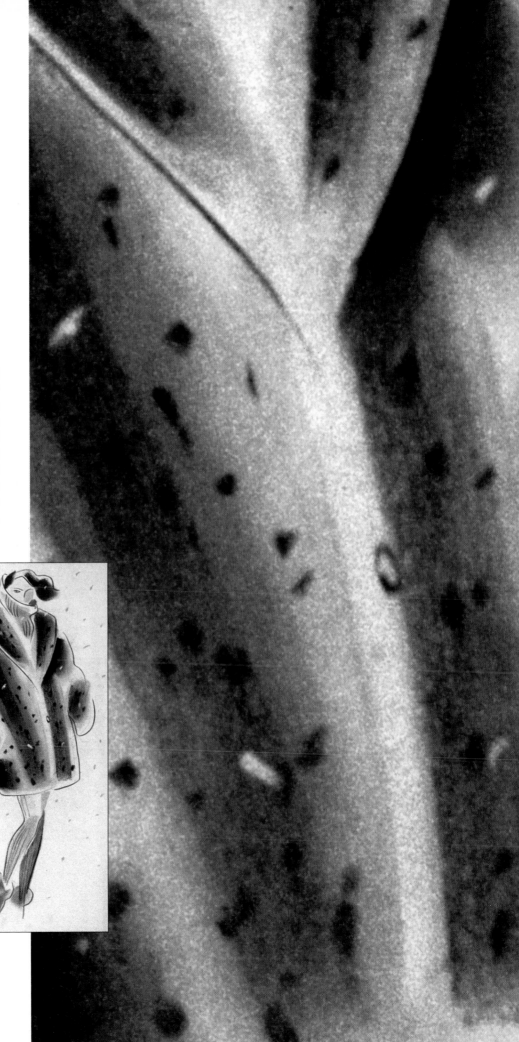

Charles Boone: Note the use of white to emphasise the herringbone weave of the jacket, which can clearly be seen in the close-up detail, although the final impression conveyed by the smaller picture is one of a grey tweed.

Charles Boone: The intricacy of detail and bright colours of the shirt's woven fabric are offset by a less formal soft pastel used for the knitwear. The essential characteristics of the two fabrics are thus conveyed by contrast.

TONE AND COLOUR VALUE EXERCISE

In drawing it is important to be selective about the choice and use of colours. Quite often new students tend to use too many colours. While full colour drawings can be lively and effective, black and white tonal drawings can be just as powerful. Indeed, a lot of fashion drawing today is reproduced in black and white. For this reason it is important to be able to reproduce in monotone the exact tonal values of a multi-coloured outfit. This simple exercise aims to show the student how to build up an image using tone and colour, first by creating a line drawing then adding tone, and finally full colour.

Stage One (left)
Take a large sheet of paper and, using a pencil, pen and ink or marker, describe the pose in linear form, using bold rather than feathery lines. Aim to cover the entire sheet.

Stage Two (above)
Using a fresh sheet of paper, draw the same or different pose in outline. Then select a tone of either black or white and add this to your drawing to accentuate highlights and add depth. As you block in the tone the quality of the drawing will change, giving it a more three-dimensional appearance. Continue building up the image in tones of black and white until the entire drawing is completely shaded in.

Stage Three (right)
Using the previous pose or selecting a new one, construct a drawing on a fresh sheet of paper, this time using full colour. Because the aim of this exercise is to help the student to understand tonal values, the choice of colours is vital. With reference to the previous drawing, choose only those colours which match the tonal values of the monochrome image. For example, where dense black is used in the previous drawing, you may wish to substitute navy blue, yellow for cream, pale blue for grey and so on.

MATERIALS

As an illustrator a wide 'palette' of materials is available to you. You should always consider the choice of medium before you start work – don't just reach for the nearest pencil and paper. Refresh your approach by making a point of experimenting with new materials occasionally.

Colin Barnes: Tempera

CHOOSING MATERIALS

Selecting materials is really a matter of personal preference. The test of a good material is one that can produce the individual quality and look which the artist aims to achieve. Experiment: buy new materials singly, and if a well-stocked art store is not within easy reach, put yourself on the mailing list of a good graphic supplier. An account costs nothing and simplifies ordering and delivery.

Paper is the first element: for everyday work, layout or drawing paper will suffice, but as experience grows, taste broadens. You may want to try the more expensive watercolour papers (made of rag), which have various textured surfaces. Try new combinations: watercolour may work well on layout paper, for example. Make yourself aware of the various papers and effects you can achieve with different materials.

Colin Barnes: Charcoal and wash. The medium gives a bold, relaxed effect, in keeping with the mood of this Richmond Cornejo suit.

Arie (right): Gouache. An illustration which demonstrates that this type of colour need not always be brilliant and poster-like. The soft coloration and a rhythm to the paint application offer attractive possibilities for the student to explore.

PENCIL

Pencil is capable of producing tight, accurate drawings, fine contour lines, soft blurred images and subtly graded areas of tone and shading. Its chief virtue is that it is so easy to correct. It is an ideal material for quick sketches, detailed drawings, and for mapping out complicated compositions on which an image can be built up in a variety of media. Coloured pencils are particularly good for adding graded areas of tone.

Do not be misled by fancy new names for old and adequate products. A pencil branded 'soft shading pencil' or 'studio pencil' is not necessarily better than the traditional carbon or lead range, graded according to hardness or softness.

For specifying instructions to a printer, a supply of mauve, blue or yellow non-print pencils are useful. Clutch pencils are excellent for fine lines and diagrammatic plans, and have the advantage of changeable leads of different thicknesses. Chinagraph and litho pencils, although designed for surfaces other than paper, produce bold marks and an interesting grainy tone. Newer pencil products are used with water to produce washes, and can be combined with drawn pencil lines.

Stavrinos (left): Pencil. Stavrinos'
highly elaborate pencil drawings
show great technical proficiency.

White

Colin Barnes (right): Pencil. This
preliminary sketch shows how an
artist working in the salon notes the
salient details for a later
composition. Shoes were registered
beside the essential line and styling
of the garment, allowing the artist as
much scope as possible for his later
refinement.

Colin Barnes:
Charcoal. This medium can be used with brush and water for washes (right). Or try combining charcoal with other materials, like collage, for contrasts and emphases (far right). It is wise to spray charcoal with a fixative before overlaying – unless of course a smudgy or 'dirty' look is positively desired.

CHARCOAL

Used in a free and gutsy manner, charcoal creates lively and expressive images. It is excellent for mapping out compositions, for bold line drawings and for adding texture, depth and shadows. Mistakes can be dusted off or removed with an eraser, and areas of tone can be blended with the finger, torchon or hand-rolled paper stumps.

Illustrators often exploit this quality of smudging and blending to effect subtle blurred tones, adding depth and movement to an image. By applying even pressure, a line of consistent width results, but interesting, jagged lines of various thicknesses can be achieved in one stroke by altering the pressure or changing the angle of the point.

Stick charcoal is made of willow or vine, in many different sizes and grades of hardness and softness. It is the purest form of charcoal and, although it snaps easily, its irregular point can be sharpened with a blade or sandpaper and gives the artist great freedom in line and tone. Compressed charcoal is made from ground powder and a binding agent. It is regular in size, less brittle, and more permanent. Even stronger is the charcoal pencil; it looks like a regular pencil and is similarly graded.

PASTELS

Chalk pastels are made from pigment mixed with wax or oil. Soft and powdery, they are sold in a wide range of colours, as sticks or pencils. They suit textured papers, good watercolour qualities or canvas as an alternative. Individual colours can be liberally applied to cover large flat areas, or more sparingly used to give delicate tints and tones, and strong, almost iridescent highlights. Try mixing colours on the paper with other chalks, or combined with charcoal, crayon, paint, conté or oil pastels.

To create smooth finishes and flat areas of tone, dust the paper surface with talcum powder and apply the pigment in even strokes using a clean cotton ball. Pigment can be gathered by scraping with a blade a small pile of dust from the end or side of a pastel stick. Lift excess dust from the drawing with tissue, and clean edges with an eraser. The dust can be mixed with solvents and applied in bold brush strokes.

Correct mistakes and pick out highlights as for charcoal drawings. Lean on a sheet of paper to protect finished areas of work and prevent smudging, and spray the artwork with a fixative at the end.

Ty Wilson (right): Pastel. Known for his strong line and simplifying technique, Ty Wilson can also bring great textural satisfaction to his fabric work.

Mouchy (left): Pastel. A treatment reminiscent of a blue mood Picasso brings out the richness and depth of the coat textile. A painterly image, using pastel crayon in a traditional manner.

87

Oil pastels create seductive tones, wonderfully suggestive colour contrasts and textures. As with all forms of illustrative work, there is nothing wrong in observing and imitating the work of masters – if it leads to a mode of expression that is all your own. Study Degas for example, who worked in pastels, creating images of magnificent quality and brilliant hues.

For oil and chalk pastels a thick watercolour paper is the most appropriate surface, although experiment with tracing or drawing paper and canvas for other effects. Try pastel on top of watercolour, or with crayons. Reverse the process: watercolour over pastels will create a broken layer, an unusual texture. Areas of smoother colour and fine washes can be built up by blending the pastels with a brush, cotton bud (Q-tip) or ball charged with oil or turpentine. Scrape thickly applied pastel from the paper with a knife or ruler to leave a flat-toned stain on the paper – now you can apply other colours, worked, overlaid or blended into the surface. Use your fingers, a cloth, a kneaded eraser, and create differing degrees of blur. Bold layers of colours are possible, or let the paper show through and add detail with a sharpened pastel, charcoal stick or pencil.

Colin Barnes (left): Pastel, with marker, on tracing paper, superimposed on a photostat textured surface. Two photographic heads have been included in this composition, the whole perfectly blended into a rich, energetic image.

Colin Barnes (above): Collage and pastel. The terracotta, earth-soft colourings, and the torn edge of the collage lend a classical quality to this head, suggesting a fragment from a sculptured frieze.

MARKERS

Hundreds of types and colours are available in fibre tip and other markers. Perhaps because it is less established, marker seems to come and go in vogue among illustrators, in comparison with other media. But developments are exciting. Pens can be used on metal, concrete, and other unusual surfaces, with nibs varying in width and shape. Colours can be laid over one another without dissolving into each other. This is useful for working on one shade close to another without fear of bleeding or combining. Flat areas of consistent colour or tone can be blocked in quickly. A wide tip is best for filling in to avoid inconsistent tone. Improvise a marker: wrap a piece of gauze or muslin around a cotton ball, secure with tape or bulldog clip and charge with fluid.

Lightweight layout paper will give soft edges and flat, semi-transparent effects, but experiment with other qualities of paper to find an individual approach.

Marker work will fade if exposed to strong ultra-violet light, but greater permanency for your work can be achieved by using a UV-retarded fixative, or a plastic laminate.

Nicole Pibeault: Marker. Not as popular now as in the seventies, marker can still be used to create images of considerable sophistication and freshness. Nicole Pibeault has exploited the vigorous, fresh colouring that felt tips can offer, but with a subtlety and looseness that suggests a more traditional medium. The woman in her illustration has a great deal of individuality, and the image contains much more than the strong fluid line for which marker has more commonly been found useful.

WATERCOLOUR

Watercolour is made from finely ground pigment mixed with gum, and is ideal for illustrations and colour reproduction. Using watercolours to achieve their characteristic transparency takes practice but once mastered, pure images of brilliant clarity and sheen are possible.

Watercolour paint is sold in pans, tubes, bottles, or you make your own with coloured pigments. Try working with a limited palette at first, mixing each one in different proportions to achieve a subtle variety of

Hippolyte Romain (above): Watercolour. An extremely strong, witty statement, quite remote from the conventional use of the material.

Pierre le Tan (right): Watercolour and ink lines. There is a very French feeling to this illustration, which is reminiscent of the etchings of Christian Bérard.

colours. Black and white can be added, but white produces the consistency of gouache, giving an opaque rather than transparent finish. This combined with watercolour is an interesting possibility.

Watercolour is mixed with other media, such as gum arabic, to thicken the paint and to use it as a watercolour varnish. Some textured papers respond better if the paint is applied to a dampened surface – use either plain water or ox gall liquid, a special wetting agent. Once watercolour is applied, mistakes are difficult to correct, but certain areas may be altered using art masking fluid which peels off, exposing clean paper. Glycerine can be mixed with the paint in order to speed up the drying process.

To lay flat wash, mix enough paint to cover the whole area. Dampen the area to be painted, and with the board held at an angle, work quickly with a brush or sponge using bold horizontal strokes. Mop up any drips or excess moisture with a soft cloth. More washes in the same or other colours can be worked into the surface while the first layer is still wet, or after it has dried. Limit the number of washes to three, otherwise the effect will dull. Or, make your wash very thin and allow the paper surface to glow through the colours. Try grading the washes by thinning the colour with water each time. Stipple it in dots, or make a texture by scrubbing with the brush in a circular motion. Combine watercolour washes with pen and ink, or add fine details with watercolour, pencil crayon or other medium, when the wash has dried.

Dry brush technique gives a different effect; load your brush, but wipe off excess moisture on a cloth before applying to the paper to produce delicate lines of separated colour. Or make a splattered surface, flicking the wetted brush at the paper. A toothbrush charged with colour can be combed or finger-fanned for a tiny spray of colour.

Colin Barnes: Watercolour and pencil. A strong image that is underlined in its success by the accuracy and conviction of the pose.

GOUACHE

Gouache is an opaque watercolour, achieved by mixing pigment with white. It can be combined with other materials and is excellent for laying flat areas of consistent colour and for using with an airbrush or stencils.

Students often find it difficult at the start to keep their colours clear and unmuddied. Try using gouache as opaquely as possible, to eliminate the white of the paper coming through. Work big, create the effect of

Roger Duncan: Gouache. A brilliant example of using gouache colour evenly and clearly, to maximum effect. This illustration is used larger than it was originally, so that the painterly quality of the work can be appreciated.

Colin Barnes (above): Gouache. A strong composition relying on clarity and balance to achieve its effect. A sporty, muscular mood is conveyed.

Colin Barnes: Gouache. For this illustration, the paint was applied thinly as a wash, almost to achieve the effect of watercolour. But the advantage of gouache is that the same colour can also be used to make small areas of intensity.

poster art. If this proves difficult, then go back to colour basics and work with collage for a while, to observe and understand the effect of flat colour areas. Crispness and clarity are the most important qualities required by the fashion illustrator, when using colour.

Mistakes are hard to correct, so sketch out a composition lightly in pencil first. Bright colours can be toned down with an eraser, and a highlight can be picked out with a toothbrush. Even a razor blade can help to remove areas of paint, provided the paper is strong enough. Alternatively, re-coat the area with a clean wet sponge or cloth, dabbing off excess moisture and repeating until most of the pigment is removed.

COLLAGE

Collage is an effective way of using flat colour, either by creating a crisp image, with neat cut-out shapes, or by exploring the more abstract possibilities of torn pieces. Very exciting tactile images can be built using three-dimensional elements, bunching up fabric or applying found objects on top of colour artwork or photographic bases. More than other techniques, collage goes in and out of fashion, and perhaps should be used sparingly. One exception to this tendency is its durability in the field of textile promotions. Fashion forecasting, fabric advertising or publicity work require excellent collage work, and offer a profitable outlet for those who enjoy this approach.

Colin Barnes (above): Paper collage. Carried out in bright colours for *Cosmopolitan* magazine. As always, accessories featured in a small page area require a composition with impact. Collage is a very effective technique in these circumstances.

Colin Barnes (right): Collage with charcoal. For a cover to *Gap* magazine, a menswear edition. Note the balance of the composition, allowing for type areas, title and strap lines, and a bold slash of yellow, vital for identity on a magazine stall.

Arie (left): Collage. Textile scraps and some gouache produce a strong, satisfying composition with tactile attraction.

Mouchy (above): This fabric collage, with gouache and an overlay, conveys texture in a fresh way.

PREPARING

for

PRINT

An illustrator needs only a reasonable store of knowledge on printing techniques as the art director usually informs the artist of the limitations which control the commission. Occasionally, there are major improvements and changes to printing methods, generally conveyed by an art director too, but an independent knowledge of these may inspire new directions in illustrative work.

Colin Barnes: Gouache used as watercolour.

THE PRINTING PROCESS

An illustrator who knows the basic processes of printing has a distinct advantage, not merely because this adds to his or her professionalism, but because it provides inspiration. Techniques can be developed using say, computer technology to distort the image, or exploring the potential of colour, tints and bleaches, or through combining positive and negative images which are capable of producing strange, surreal imagery and colour contrasts.

Most commercial printing is now done using the 'Offset Litho' method. 'Offset' refers to the method of printing: an inked image held in a metal plate is printed onto a rubber blanket wrapped round a metal cylinder. This in turn rotates and the image is transferred from the rubber blanket to the paper. The rubber protects the surface of the litho plate and avoids the damage that could occur if the plate came into direct contact with coarse paper surfaces. Rubber's flexibility compensates for the irregularities of different surfaces and it can be used for printing on a wide variety of surfaces, including metal itself. Offset litho is fast, inexpensive and capable of producing high-quality colour work in fine detail. Sophisticated multi-colour machines can run several colours at one pass-through, so that the final image can be seen immediately.

For print, line, or colour to be transferred to paper, the original artwork has to be photographed by a process camera, which turns the image into a negative print. By far the easiest and cheapest method is to reproduce black and white line originals which contain no half-tones. To capture variations of light and shade in a black and white original the photographic negative is broken up into a series of tiny dots. The dots represent the areas of light in the image and therefore the darker the tone the greater the density of dots. The lighter the tone, the lower the density.

Colour reproductions are more complicated and expensive to print. The original artwork has to be broken down into the basic primary components. Four separate printing plates are made, one for each colour, which are represented in the printing process by using yellow for the yellow areas, magenta for the red, cyan for the blue, and black. By using these four in different combinations and varying degrees of intensity more or less any colour can be reproduced.

Colour half-tones can be reproduced by using a half-tone screen for

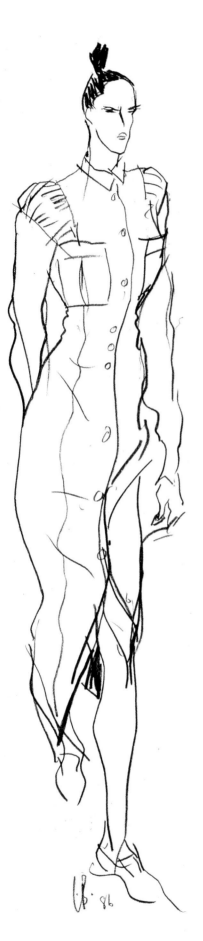

Colin Barnes: Simple line drawings, like this rendering of a Richmond Cornejo design, are often required for newspaper work.

each colour. Each screen is made up of parallel lines which when superimposed at different angles intersect to form a rosette pattern. Although the entire image is printed as a series of overlapping dots, at normal reading distance these become invisible and are impossible to distinguish when the image is printed at the correct size. Colour separation is done either by the process camera, using different filters to separate out each colour component or, more commonly, by a laser scanner which is more accurate and takes less time. In this method the image is scanned by a high-intensity light or laser beam which is directed via colour filters and a computer. This automatically produces individual screen films for each colour component, in positive or negative to order. Separate plates are then made from them.

Most artwork for magazines or books will be printed four-colour – that is, cyan, magenta, yellow and black – the 'process colours'. Sometimes 'special' colours may be specified which cannot be mixed from the process colours. This will require a 'special working' so that the job is run through the press an extra time. Some jobs are printed in one colour only – say a Pantone red, with solid colours, tints of red and white.

There are endless different printing processes, combinations and permutations, continually being added to and improved upon as new technology comes into being alongside the existing methods. A wealth of specialist literature on the subject appears, which the illustrator should consult from time to time to be sure to keep up with what is possible. Consult the client or the production department concerned so that you know what kind of paper is being used, the limitations of the method in hand, the number and variations of colours available, and so on. There is no substitute for the occasional visit to a printing works, to see the machinery in action and to know what the difficulties are on the ground floor. This makes the job of printing very real, and with each commission completed, your understanding of the possibilities grows richer.

PREPARING ARTWORK FOR REPRODUCTION

An illustrator always starts with as specific a brief as he or she can gather. This does not concern the nature of the image alone, but the type of information it will convey, the style and amount of text accompanying it,

THE FOUR-COLOUR PROCESS

Colour separations: Incredible as it appears, all colour work in commercial printing is made up of four basic colour inkings, or four plates, using yellow, magenta for red, cyan for blue, and black. By using these in various intensities and combinations most colours can be achieved. Corrections are made by adjusting the colour inkings of the plates.

Werner: This finished version of the separations opposite gives some idea of the subtlety that four-colour printing can offer. The greatest problem is one of registration – getting the four plates to sit one on top of the other accurately. The possibilities for error are considerable, but fine effects, such as the transparency of the fabric shown here, can be reproduced with subtle definition.

David Downton (above): Brush and ink. This illustration is reproduced in half-tone, which allows for greater range in the shades from pure black through various greys.

Zoltan (right): Collage. Three-dimensional collage work may not be suitable for the reproduction process used by the printing house. Illustrators must always check that their work is in an appropriate physical form. In this instance, problems are avoided by creating a photographic image of the collage, without losing the three-dimensional depth.

the kind of readership aimed at, the format and size of the reproduction, and last but not least the particular method and quality of the printing. All this will vary from one job to another. (See pages 128–9 for more information on briefs and taking on commissions.)

A good brief will specify the final size and format of the printed reproduction. If it does not, it is essential to confirm these facts; they help you to determine the scale of the original artwork and the technique to be employed. With every new commission, make sure the employer knows and agrees to your method of working, to avoid misunderstandings as much as possible.

Drawing larger and smaller than the actual size of reproduction means you must be able to gauge the change of effect that will result. A very large drawing can lose impact when reproduced on a smaller scale; on the other hand, oversize drawing may enable you to put in detail that is difficult to achieve working on a lesser scale. Many artists use overscale or miniature purposefully, as a way of achieving or enhancing a particular effect. Within reason reduced images can make colours appear more solid, details and lines crisper. Blown-up images can soften hues and give an interestingly textured, grainy look (while also losing clarity and detail). Experiments, practice, and experience builds up your repertoire.

The most common sizes used for artwork are scaling the image 'half-up' (one and a half times up) or twice the size of the reproduced image. Reductions or enlargements are calculated on a percentage scale, e.g. a reduction from 80 mm to 60 mm is 25%. An easy way to work out scale in percentages is to use the formula: the size of the reproduced image divided by the size of the original (times 100).

CHOOSING MATERIALS

Of course materials and techniques are usually determined by the subject matter, the size of reproduction and the print process, or they may be specified by the client. It is sensible to check all this with the client first – particularly where certain print processes have limitations that require you to avoid particular colours or techniques. In general, bold black and white line drawings look good on poor quality paper such as newsprint, whereas delicate half-tones, fine pencil lines and subtle tints will benefit

Zoltan

from being printed on a smoother, less textured surface. Magazines tend to stick to the same stock, but it is as well to check in other fields, such as book or brochure publishing, where a variety of papers may be under consideration for the job.

All work should be pasted up onto a flexible board or drawn directly onto it, for most laser colour scanning requires it to be wrapped round a drum shape. This is a quick method but has its limitations: some colours are difficult to reproduce well, and artwork executed in thick layers of paint and delicate collage may crack or tear in the process. Quite often an illustrator is told to present several small images together on one board, to save money on reproduction: obviously it is important to fix these down well so they do not peel up when fitted to the drum. (Cow gum, rubber cement or a similar product is used because individual bits of work can be lifted off or repositioned at will without risk of damage to the paper.)

Colin Barnes: Here, an overlay,
featuring powerful strokes of white,
was used to give a particular relief
on the figure drawings.

OVERLAYS

Overlays are sometimes used for colour separation, as a means of sending instructions to the printer, or simply to protect the artwork. Learn the language of printing instructions, such as 'square up' (centre on the page area), 'cut out' (extract image from background) or 'cut into' (place inside or overlapping another image) and make sure you understand all terms under discussion on any job. Cover yourself by writing all important instructions on a slip of paper attached to the back of the artwork with tape. Quite often these will be repeated for the printer by the art department, but if your own are correct, it saves time and prevents difficulties later.

Modern processing machinery has almost done away with the need for separate overlays for each colour. In four colour artwork the only overlay required is for type, usually but not always black. It is separate because it will not be screened as artwork. If the work is to be printed in one language only the line work can be printed with the type, but if it is to be published abroad or if the same colourwork is to be used in a different edition, (say with much reduced text for a cheaper book) the text and line is kept separate so that a new black plate can be produced easily, without the colour being altered in any way. Overlays are also used for type or line which is to be printed in one of the process colours, or type or line which is to be reversed out of colour, or again, for areas to be reproduced as tints or a 'special' colour. If you want to use mechanical tints, popular for newspaper work, specify them for the reproduction house or apply them yourself. Registration marks indicate how overlays fit together.

CORRECTING MISTAKES

The easiest method of correcting work is to redraw the part to size and paste it up over the top. The outline does not normally show when the image is photographed. This is a cleaner and better technique than masking out the image with white paint or redrawing the whole thing. Layouts should always be carefully cleaned up – otherwise, thumbprints or rough lines will reproduce. Easily smudged work, such as pastel, charcoal and graphite is sprayed with a fixative. Positioning lines are made in light blue, which does not show up on the film negative.

PROFESSIONAL WORK

There are many aspects to illustrative work, from editorial, advertising, through professional brochures, to posters. Initially, as a new artist, you will only manage a small amount of editorial commissions; only through published jobs can art directors become aware of your abilities and make the first approach. It takes a few years to build up work. During this period you may find an agent and familiarise yourself with the pitfalls that attend all freelance activities.

Colin Barnes: Watercolour

THE FASHION WORLD

Fashion is a growing and diverse industry. It encompasses much more than the designer and the makers of clothes, cutters and machinists. There are machinery designers, pattern cutters, manufacturers with their own buyers (for textiles and trimmings, and people who make just these) forecasting companies servicing the manufacturers, photographers, film-makers, advertisers, models, stylists, marketing companies, package designers – and illustrators.

Designers need to draw, but they do so for a completely different purpose from the illustrator. Designers conceive the style and silhouette, convey structural details for the pattern cutter, manufacturer and sample maker, and give fabric information. The illustrator, on the other hand, makes commercial visuals to sell the finished product. The market dictates the style of illustration; the artist has to get the message across in details, in the mood, the style, and in his unique method of execution.

It is not enough to be able to draw: an illustrator has to know the whole business, love the work, be alert to changes and have an obsession with fashion. Very few illustrators become famous overnight — very few become famous at all, and only a small number make a livelihood! And anyone going into the profession must be prepared to take time to learn skills, understand what is needed and most importantly, know how to produce it. Go to the events; be a spy; notice what is happening on the catwalks; read all the magazines; wander round the stores; examine the new clothes; study the displays; visit art galleries; watch television and sketch in the street. The learning process for the illustrator never ceases.

Above all, recognise from the start that a lot of the work is going to be routine, pedestrian and essential. For every glorious piece of self-expression there will be days of utter boredom executing routine jobs. Outlets vary and the illustrator has to get into all of them.

EDITORIAL—GLOSSY MAGAZINES

Magazines cover all areas of the market, in all manner of combinations: pure fashion, fashion with cookery/fiction/interviews/home ideas, and so on. This broad editorial range gives illustrators the chance to create stylish and imaginative visuals; an enterprising art director may give a new illustrator a chance, if original work is on offer. But it may not be

Pierre le Tan (above): Watercolour. A restrained use of colour focuses interest in the mood and character of the clothes.

Zoltan (left): Photographic collage. A single colour is used to great effect, achieving a depth of image which gives a strong tactile element to the composition.

Colin Barnes: Series of illustrations for a menswear feature. Although commissions for entire editorial spreads are difficult to come by, an illustrator should always be capable of coming up with some theme or idea to make a collection of garments work in an interesting visual layout. Sometimes the treatment of the spread may originate with the art director, at other times the illustrator may be given more freedom.

Anyone preparing a portfolio would be advised to work up some ideas to a fairly high state of completion, so that art directors can see imagination and originality realised. Gradually pieces that have been prepared just for presentation are replaced by commissioned material. The ideal portfolio contains a range of images from initial thoughts to finished concepts.

119

Colin Barnes: Charcoal. This illustration was commissioned for a newspaper advertisement. Black and white newsprint is not the subtlest of forms, and calls for a vigorous use of the space allotted.

quite as grand as wished for. More and more magazines cram in as much on a page as is possible, with only a few sacrificing a whole page for fashion illustration.

Noteworthy areas of expansion are in the coverage of major fashion shows and the treatment of beauty features. For established illustrators there is plenty of scope; a beginner often has to work to precise briefs with layouts generally already decided by the art directors.

High gloss magazines have a lot of money in their budget; although little of it reaches the pocket of the illustrator there is prestige and spin-off from getting your work accepted by a top quality publication. It often compensates for poor payment. But it is not easy to get that important first commission. Big names impress; favourites rule the roost (not just because they are known but because what they do is familiar, well-liked and comes in reliably). But competition between the magazines provides one way to unlock the door: being one step ahead is the key to success in the fashion business. Your portfolio may provide a new trend in design and be taken up – another strong reason to keep an eye on what is happening in the fashion world, at home and abroad.

EDITORIAL—NEWSPAPERS

Newspapers now operate very similarly to magazines, occasionally using illustration for accessory stories, and seldom commissioning a full fashion drawing. If used, the drawing has to be executed in strong black line and very little tone.

Occasionally, as an alternative to photography, a witty and amusing line drawing may be used, almost to capture some of the old atmosphere of 'couture reports'. Gone are the days when the illustrator accompanied the fashion editor to major shows, memorised the best models and reproduced them instantly as soon as he or she had left the salon, without any further references.

TRADE JOURNALS

Trade publications such as *Womenswear Daily, Sir International,* Italian and French *Gap* are all regarded as gospel for current news on fashion trends internationally. Trade publications are numerous and offer good openings for new illustrators and constant well-paid work for the more established. While the need is to express garment style, details and fabric textures, editorial diversity allows for some individual interpretation. Close study of all these publications to gain knowledge of their likes and dislikes is invaluable.

Arie: Acrylic. Trade journals require precision and clarity, although Italian *Gap*, for which these illustrations were done, is freer in interpretative requirements than the Paris edition. A subtle use of colour makes these images very distinctive.

IC CHIC ... LYCRA 1988 – EROTIC CHIC ... LYCRA 1988 – EROTIC CHIC ... LYCRA 1988 – EROTIC CHIC ... LYCRA 1988 – EROTIC CHIC ... LYCRA 1988 – EROTIC CHIC ... LYCRA 1988 – EROTIC CHIC ...   1

ADVERTISING

More clothes are sold through advertising than through editorial copy; the advantage here is that the client controls the look of his product. But the competition is not only between the photographer and the fashion illustrator – it takes in graphic designers, cartoonists and other specialist artists as well. Undoubtedly a lucrative area, it is also a highly

Hélène Tran (right): Gouache and line. An energetic composition. The finished reproduction may be considerably smaller or larger than the artwork, and this must be allowed for in the treatment of the image.

Viramontes (right): A store promotion poster.

competitive and limited one, with the best work going to proven professionals. However, novelty is vital to the business, so it is worth being very positive and persevering.

Newspaper advertisement does use illustration to some extent. Again, as in editorial page work, strong line is used because it creates impact. The quality of printing and the pressure on space does not allow much detail or information to be conveyed in any other medium.

Major department stores use illustration to convey the corporate image and information in the absence of made-up samples. Advertising in magazines, newspapers and trade journals, packaging, posters, customer mailouts, and illustration for swing tickets, displays and other in-store promotional material are all part of the artist's potential brief.

Being the major selling point for fashion and cosmetic companies, stores also require illustrated brochures, storyboards for videos and commercials from the manufacturers to be screened in various departments. Each area requires specialised art skills. There is no shortage of work (a large part of which is commissioned by the various manufacturing companies themselves or their advertising or marketing agents).

This kind of work often calls for poster art – rather different in its style and impact from purely editorial artwork. Some large manufacturing companies distribute their images internationally. Copyright is usually retained by the artist and payment made on a royalty basis.

The various stores' public relations personnel give information about the work structure, such as whether all illustration commissions are dealt with by in-house staff, farmed out, or handled through subsidiaries.

PRINTEMPS

PRINTEMPS
LE PLUS
PARISIEN
DES GRANDS
MAGASINS

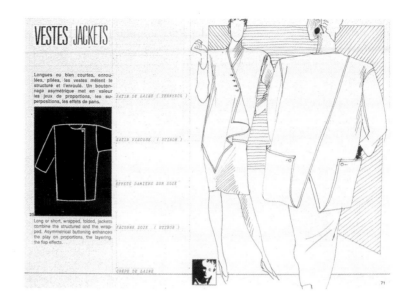

Mouchy: These paste-up boards are part of a fashion forecast commission. Mouchy combined her illustrative work with the textual layout of the pages.

FORECASTING

Fashion forecasters serve an international market. Working with major retailers and high street stores, they advise on future styles, fabrics, colours and product design, providing reports tailored to individual clients. To produce accurate, reliable fashion forecasting they also travel the world clipping ideas from the fashion circuit. Consultancies work closely with fibre producers, textile mills, accessories and cosmetic firms. Often working up to twenty months in advance of the retail business, forecasters call on the services of other specialists, researchers, market analysts, and illustrators, to get the 'trends' across to their customers.

Most forecasting companies have a staff team of designers and illustrators but also employ freelancers. This work provides a large proportion of commissions for fashion illustrators. But there is little scope for individual interpretation. The job is to turn out hundreds of flatplans to tight specifications. These show accurate proportional details which can be read easily by marketeers and manufacturers. Conventional, almost diagrammatic presentation is necessary. The challenge lies in conveying a concept pictorially, without seeing the actual garment.

The yearly cycle of a top company involves a rigid schedule, with each facet running concurrently – men's, women's, children's wear, accessories and so on. A typical scheme for men's wear predictions would begin in February with forecast details of lines for the Spring/Summer season of the following year, and update information on fabrics, colours and merchandising concepts. Design manuals are published in March containing graphics and literature on fabrics, accessories and promotional

items. Current 'hot' news is circulated in April. May is taken up with yarn reports and photos of European fabrics and yarn fairs. The latest trends from the top European resorts are illustrated in photopacks in July. In August and September forecasts are made for Autumn/Winter of the following year with colour predictions for the Spring/Summer of the year after, plus a design manual and 'newsflash' updating future key items. The European market is reviewed in October, with illustrations and comment on the designer collections and, again, forecasts for the following Spring. Finally, November covers fabric and yarn fairs.

Anyone interested in this area of the fashion business is well advised to study the output from a number of the major companies. Illustration in a conventional, reliably successful style tends to be favoured.

CLOTHING PATTERNS

Although photography has made inroads in the presentation of paper pattern styles, illustration is still widely used for both the store catalogues and individual packages. Generally, garment designs and their patterns are created and made up in house. The toile is given to the freelance illustrator whose first task is to provide a pencil sketch showing the outline silhouette, with basic structural details. Adjustment to drawing, suggesting alternative poses or correction of details are made by the pattern company. The work is then 'swatched' and returned to the illustrator with the toile for the artwork to be completed. Accompanying diagrammatic flat plans are usually produced by in-house designers. As with forecasting work, the style of illustration is conventional and precise.

125

SETTING UP IN BUSINESS

Colin Barnes (above): Watercolour and pencil. This was executed for an editorial feature in *Gap*.

Not all illustrators are able to identify from the start their area of specialisation. Indeed, there are many who choose to be diverse. Being confined to one area can be advantageous if you are fortunate to choose a type of work that is in constant demand, such as fashion forecasting or clothing patterns. But the drawback is that you can become too limited, and when the tide turns, unprepared for finding work elsewhere.

The same applies to a portfolio. It is unhelpful to show a collection of flat diagrammatic drawings to a client whose marketing needs call for a loose, flamboyant approach. Although a degree of versatility is needed, it is better to start out by developing a strong, recognisable style.

BUILDING A PORTFOLIO

Preparing a portfolio is actually very similar to laying out a magazine page. Avoid things that clash too badly, show off individual samples of your work with plenty of 'air' – if one drawing is tiny, mount it on a big empty page so that it looks valued. Always use clean boards, and have your work well laid down. All attachments and mounts must be professional looking. At the beginning drawn work will probably fill the whole book; later, printed examples of work should always be included and be as handsomely presented as original artwork.

A fashionable appearance and an air of self-confidence is persuasive. However, examining the work of better known illustrators leads more to the conclusion that their success is fuelled repeatedly by their ability to surprise and inspire, through creating original and imaginative work, over and over again – servicing not only the top end of the market, but every level with the best ideas for what is needed. On this basis, the aim of any artist should be constantly to provide newly conceived visuals which reflect the mood and lifestyle of the moment. It is this element which should be uppermost in mind when visiting a potential client with a portfolio of work.

THE CLIENT'S REQUIREMENTS

The top professionals may disagree in detail but in the main share the same response: whatever the outlet, it is not enough to be able to draw the figure, however well. To be effective a drawing needs 'style and flair'. One

or two individuals complain vehemently that presentation is often poor. Others believe that a work's character and power shines through whether displayed in glossy plastic or a shabby cardboard file.

The difficulty in identifying what a client wants is that styles and trends are so transitory that what appears fashionable one month may be old-hat the next. Illustrators are misled if they think they will do better with a selection of derivative work than an honest body of their own material. Nothing is ever static in the arts. Lawrence Mynott, who considers himself more as a general illustrator than a fashion artist (but whose work is certainly original) says, 'I am often asked to do something "in the style of . . . ." and in the past I have made quite a profession of being a sort of plagiarist because the only way some people can evoke a style is to copy it slavishly.'

Whether your bent is towards flat diagrammatic drawings or elaborate renderings, follow your own instincts. To inspire confidence: it is quality and not quantity that counts. Make some effort to create strong work, especially for your portfolio, and update it regularly. 'If I see twenty drawings and only two are outstanding, how can I be sure that in a commission I would be the lucky one to get the right drawing?' queries Malgosia Szemberg, Assistant Art Director for *Elle* UK.

Lawrence Mynott (above):
Gouache. A pastiche of the Gruau style of fashion illustration (see page 22), with a theatricality not unlike the work of Lautrec.

FINDING WORK

Basic sensible steps apply as in any freelance occupation. Type your correspondence; have a stock of printed resumés and business cards to hand out whenever needed; order personalised notepaper, and as soon as you can afford it, an answerphone for messages. (Later on, a computer or word processor will store your files, and your ideas.)

Compile a comprehensive list of possible sources of work and ask everyone you know for their additions – especially those with precise details on certain companies. Find out as much as you can about any company before making contact.

Maurice Arrari: Rapidograph. A catwalk sketch, catching all the salient details for working up to a finished illustration.

COMMISSIONS AND BRIEFS

The commission from an art director client or agent will include the brief. This conveys quickly and precisely the idea, format and time schedule for

delivery. It is the illustrator's task to fulfil the brief strictly according to specification. It is quite common for a beginner to be asked to do trial work before a real commission is given. You may not be paid for it, but it is usually worth the effort, if only for the experience. But then, one distinguished art director warns, 'an illustrator should know when to refuse a job, and if he accepts a job he should understand what is expected. It's no use saying, "I don't draw that way" – if you can't, don't take the job.'

Be sure to get all relevant details spelt out in the commission. The budget (who pays for materials, hire of models if needed, transport and delivery?), the time schedule and fees (how much and to whom should the bill be sent, and in the event of rejection, what sum will be paid?). Check very carefully on format – the size required; how the work should be mounted; the reproduction process; if separations are required, and if roughs are needed. Finally, copyright: who will own the finished artwork?

The scale of your enquiries and efforts should match the project. Do not waste time on elaborate roughs if the client only requires a simple job.

AGENTS

It is always difficult to decide whether agents earn their money or not, and at what point in any career it is worth considering outside help. Unless an artist shows particular promise, most agents will not consider taking on anyone straight from college. They too want to maximise their efforts by handling only clients who are established, with a good portfolio, and a strong likelihood of future work. This leads inevitably to the conclusion that if you can get on a long way through your own efforts, you are unlikely to progress even further with an agent's help. There has to be a mutual benefit: maybe the agent has contacts in a whole new area?

Look carefully at what an agent offers in terms of promotion. Some upmarket agents offer a substantial range of goods, including calendars, bound booklets or 'packs' and a selection of advertisements and free listings in trade journals and directories. The artefacts are distributed to all commissioning clients, magazines and design groups. This is not, however, a service free of charge. Find out exactly the split between agent and artist, and how the deduction is made.

Colin Barnes: A quick sketch drawn in a styliste's *atelier,* with references to accessories and all details.

Christopher Brown: Linocut. This shows a completely novel treatment of a figure, reminiscent of European folk art in its decorative elements.

Of course agents help with a variety of other services: finding work, negotiating contracts, conveying briefs to illustrators, hiring models, and chasing up payments! Look for someone who is experienced in all areas of management, public relations and marketing. A secondary decision is whether to go to someone who specialises in fashion illustrators or with artists in other fields too. You may be in direct competition with another of your agent's clients.

COPYRIGHT

'Artlaw' is highly specialised, and ranges across the many artistic disciplines. There are some guidelines to keep in mind, but in the event of any real problem, always consult a lawyer specializing in art law.

Copyright owners are given by law the exclusive right to grant permission to others to use their work in reproduction, publishing, broadcasting or film – any or all of these rights in a combination will be specified in the contract.

The Copyright Acts of 1956 (UK) and 1976 (USA) set out which works can be so protected, and for how long. Different protection is given for different works, depending on how the work was created.

Copyright protection is given to artistic works only if they are 'original' – that is, unique – not a derived copy of someone else's work. 'Artistic work' includes paintings, drawings, prints, sculpture, architectural works, maps and charts and drawings for industrial design.

The length of time this protection covers in general is, 'the artist's lifespan plus fifty years'.

Usually the creator owns the copyright, but there are exceptions here too, notably in commissioned work (work-for-hire), where the commissioner of a work or an employer may own the copyright unless a contract between the parties specifically states that the artist will do so. The only way to know your own position is to have your contracts checked by any agent involved and a lawyer.

A copyright owner can sell rights to the work. Rights must be signed over in writing, with the owner's signature. Usually this is transacted for a reasonable fee or royalty. An artist can issue a license for the temporary use of an image. It is not legally necessary to put such an agreement in writing but it is good business practice to do so.

It is always advisable to keep a clear copy of your work – a transparency or photograph – in the event of disputes.

Sometimes your work is used without permission, infringing your copyright. This is unlawful and entitles the copyright holder to sue for payment of any profit made by the infringer, and to stop further abuses. There are sensible exceptions, where copyright works are used for private study, criticism, review or reporting of current events, but these must always carry an acknowledgement of the source, title and copyright ownership details.

Always sign your work with the international copyright symbol, a 'c' encircled, your name, and the year date. In the UK, extra protection and support can be found in joining the Designers and Copyright Society (DACS). For further information for the USA, contact the Graphic Artists Guild or the Copyright Office in Washington D.C.

ORGANISING REFERENCE MATERIAL

Like all creative artists, fashion illustrators find inspiration and renewal from a range of sources. The pressure is on them to be inventive, so it is helpful to have a variety of material at hand to trigger the imagination.

Clippings from magazines and newspapers are best arranged chronologically, filed in cardboard boxes, plastic wallets or ringbinders. It may seem a chore to mark the date and the publication on each cutting, and any other useful information – the name of the designer, illustrator, photographer and so on – but it is amazing how often you need to know.

Visits to museums can be more permanently useful if you buy postcards – a constant source of inspiration and a cheap substitute for expensive catalogues. A sketchbook always to hand serves well, particularly when photography is forbidden.

Try to keep a good record of all your work, in transparencies, and add the medium used, the date, and who made the commission.

Keep a pressbook of published work and any reviews as a useful back-up to your portfolio of current work. Always date your rejected or experimental work too – sometimes a quiet, critical review of past ideas adds to your self-knowledge, and can spur you in a new creative direction.

Jean Paul Raymond: A Gauguin-like pose matches the naive treatment of the patterning, but the use of colours is subtle and sophisticated, in keeping with the clothes by Kenzo.

131

THE GALLERY

The essential quality of
fashion, and therefore of
fashion illustration, is that
just as you are accustomed
to a look or a line, the whole
mood changes – and the
illustrator must be able to
reflect that change.
All magazines and papers
could do with livening up,
having whole pages
presenting drawings, not
an apology of an illustration
in a corner. The newness,
the freshness that artwork
can produce should be
encouraged.

Colin Barnes: Watercolour

ARIE

❝ *My drawing in acrylic was for an editorial feature in* Gap *Italy; in common with many of my drawings, it contains the elements of elimination or exaggeration which I like to employ. Illustration is not a record of fact, like photography. You can bring some other quality to the representation of the image, something unique and individual, with such devices. I use acrylic a lot, also pastel, and collage work from time to time also.*

My art college training covered both fashion design and illustration. I like both activities, but I decided that for me, illustration work would be more creative, less obviously commercial, and at that time, when I started out, there were less people in illustration than in fashion.

In particular I prefer quick sketch work. I enjoy capturing fast movement, and finding some way to typecast the outfit I am seeing, in a few seconds. This can be done for high-fashion collections, for instance. I like it perhaps because it allows for the greatest freedom of artistic expression. ❞

MAURICE ARRARI

6 *Insofar as the term 'fashion' also connotes 'attitude', I have always tried to evoke in my illustrations the way the individual should feel when wearing certain proportions and textures, certain colours, and how these should influence the way a person projects his body and gestures in the space around him; the sort of character the current 'fashion' portrays him to be.*

This picture was publicity work for Vogue *magazine, and is characteristic of the work I like to do. I enjoy conveying the texture of fabric, especially transparency, so that we still feel the body. My work owes a lot to painting, especially to artists like Lautrec and Degas who loved to portray performers and dancers and who taught me that gesture betrays character. I studied dance movement for many years.*

Without a 'stance' or 'attitude', fashion – and all the more so illustration of that fashion – becomes insipid and carries no particular message which could provoke you to sit up and take notice. **9**

ROGER DUNCAN

6 *It is interesting that this picture has
been selected as it was one of the first commissions I did for
Madame Figaro in Paris, an editorial spread, and it contains
many of the significant features of my illustration work. I did ten
pages for them, this was the leading page.*

*I have a fine arts background, but fashion illustration has
always fascinated me, because I see fashion as a form of
communication. Sculpting oneself in clothing. You get up feeling
sour or good, and dress accordingly; illustrating the mood of
clothing is to me a form of communication, like writing. I like to
work with live models, because they touch the clothes, arrange them
in ways which come naturally and help me to see the character of
the clothing.*

*Recent couture collections have been full of great colour and
shapes, short skirts, beautiful big hats. Personally, I like fall
clothes, the texture of fur . . . I have a strong sense of taste – of
course sometimes one is faced with items that are difficult to draw
because they may not be wonderful. But you must adapt to the
situation. A client may depend on you to come up with a mood,
give the flavour of their clothes, and really open up the image.*

*Looking at clothes on the catwalk is the ultimate reality. You
see something moving, making a new shape. At first I was
frightened of drawing from the catwalk, in case I got a terrific new
line, say the jacket swinging open, and forgot where the buttons
were! But gradually my scribbles became more expressive of the
essence of the garment – and I can say that often the briefest
drawing will be accepted if it does that.* **9**

PIERRE LE TAN

6 *Here is a simple drawing, pen and
ink and gouache, for a 1982 Kenzo design. Nowadays I use more
brush and ink, because it is quicker, and suits my mood – or just as
often, the deadline.
I don't find it all that easy to get down to work, so I tend
to do it at the last minute. It's not that I have difficulty
with the inspiration, but I am lazy. Of course some jobs are
nice to do, and some are deadly, although you can usually
find a way to make the clothes look good. I doubt if starting
work earlier would have any effect on the quality of the
work that I do; it is always hard.* **9**

SHARON LONG

6 *My illustration was an entry in the
Benson and Hedges Competition, 'Style'. It is a Comme des
Garcons outfit, and I chose it because at that time the peplum was
making a comeback and it was a good example of a new line, or
silhouette. I am bad at drawing things I don't like, so I do tend to
be given the more avant-garde clothes as they are more complex,
and there's more to draw, more to grasp.*

*I work very big – larger than A1-size sheets, and I draw from
life always. This can be a great problem when starting as a
fashion illustrator. Finding good bodies as volunteers may be
difficult, and in my case I work fairly slowly, so I take up people's
time. I like my faces to have character, and these too I draw from
life. Sometimes I can see a face clearly, but it is hard to get exactly
what I want without a model who comes close to it.*

*There is not a vast amount of fashion work around; I consider
myself a general illustrator. I do many other commissions, for
example book jackets. Currently I'm working with collage,
pastel, oil pastel, a mixture, but I expect to turn to other
materials in the future. You must never stop making changes in
your work, otherwise you get bored.* **9**

LAWRENCE MYNOTT

❦ *This illustration, in torn paper
collage, was for* The Observer *newspaper, so the colour had
nothing to do with it; it was meant to be slight tones of grey. My
reason for using this technique was that Paris reportage is a
nightmare: you have to do it in a day. The clothes that season were
very short, structured, very directional, and I wanted to get across
the immediacy of the situation. 'Short sharp shock' was the caption
to this picture. Torn paper was good for that.*

*Fashion is to me a social statement, not out on a limb, but
related to other aesthetic changes, in architecture, furniture. I am
not primarily a fashion artist – I approach it as a stylistic
exercise. You have to match the technique to the medium. In certain
instances, illustrators have conveyed the mood of a designer so well
that we think of them inseparably – like Gruau and Dior.*

*The rhythm of the figure is very important to me, and
photography cannot cope with its changes. Actually, photography
can be deceptive, suggest a floaty fabric when it is in reality stiff.
As a student I used to like going to the zoo to practise. It is good
training getting movement and character – particularly if you
watch fine, beautiful animals, elegant gazelles, antelopes, leopards.
It teaches you a lot about proportion, angles, the axis of a body,
and the movement of animals' markings is wonderful to observe.*

*I do not work to a formula. I don't have one style,
like the couturiers who do their own drawings – Lacroix
for example has this 'illustrator' look in his work. I just
try for an imaginative statement. Like the tailors
who cut the cloth to suit the fabric . . .* ❧

MICHAEL ROBERTS

❛ I studied fine art originally at High Wycombe, followed by graphics and then fashion. I have worked as a fashion journalist, a fashion illustrator and now I'm more interested in photography and film work – moving images interest me a lot at the moment. But I still do all three, I like a mixture.

I don't have a particular style, I tend to suit the treatment to the subject matter, though I suppose there has always been a theme, a sort of flat, découpage, Fauvist, Matissey look. I used to do a lot of Art Deco style work too. But if I'm drawing an Edelstein ballgown, then I might go for an early Hartnell, fifties look.

I think fashion illustration is about interpreting clothes. I like to emphasize, enlighten the observer with what the clothes are about. I do not have to work with very good clothes particularly, in fact I positively like illustrating terrible clothes, where photography would be a dead giveaway and illustration can bring out the best in them. I get a response to the clothes, more than requiring a special outlet to work for.

Fashion illustration is enjoying a renaissance at the moment. There are lots of good people at work in Europe and, in the UK, magazines are beginning to mix up photography and illustration, giving both equal place on some pages. As clothes become more fantastic, fashion illustration serves better to capture the mood. In fact, some clothes, such as Lacroix, almost look better in illustration than in real life – very few people wear them successfully. But as indicators of what is to come, as an influence on fashion, as images, these clothes are important. ❜

STAVRINOS

❝ *I studied graphics at college, but I
was always drawing in pencil, throughout my childhood. When I
left college and developed my portfolio I found that the graphite
work was taking over the rest, so I just threw everything else out.
With pencil I get the most immediate form of what I want to do. I
have more control than with painting, water, and so on, and I get
sharp detail.*

*This illustration was a commission from a New York store,
Nordstroms, who were having an exhibition on 'Things to Come'
in furniture, design, fashion and so on. I was asked to contribute
ideas about fashion – note the radio concealed in the girl's hat.
Underneath the softness of her garment there is a real, or maybe
artificial construction. Who knows what the future will bring . . .*

*I fell into fashion – I didn't really study or train for it. It is a
challenge for me, as I did not start out with that focus. But then
one of the classes I liked best during my training was life class, so
the figure work always interested me.*

My work does involve painstaking detail – for a New York
Times *drawing I guess I work three days and nights. I tend to do
a lot of sketches, before the final. I can't knock it out, I have to
work very hard to get that patina, the finished look. I would be no
good at the catwalk! In that life class at school, I remember some
advice we were given: 'put yourself in the drawing', so I really try
to feel the fabric, the touch of velvet, get involved in it. I think this
approach helped me to become more accomplished as I continued
with it. My aim is to make the surface of any picture really
seductive, so that you want to touch it.* ❞

PHAN VAN MY

❛ *I am Vietnamese, I have always lived in Paris and I love it. I studied History of Art at the Sorbonne, but I knew I wanted to work in fashion. For a year I was 'accessoriste' with Ted Lapidus, meanwhile I worked on my portfolio hoping that I would move into illustration work before long. Now I am known for fashion illustration, but like any freelance artist I do many other commissions, in advertising, promotion and so on – funnily enough, I am often asked to give a computer ad, a cruise liner or a frozen trout picture, a 'fashion type' look! I think my work is very 'French', and international clients like that. Another area I enjoy is illustrating children's books, but the market in France is very small for this.*

If I say I like certain people, I am not suggesting I am in the same category. Nor is my interest in them out of nostalgia, or a desire to replicate their work, but for inspiration. My idol is Antonio. I believe every fashion illustrator owes a great deal to him. An influential figure was A. M. Cassandre (a designer of posters and typography in the thirties). Naturally, I also admire the work of the greatest painters, Picasso and Matisse, because above everything else I adore colour. Why work in black and white, when there's so much colour? Black and white is for literature! I love light colours, though I have never ever worked in watercolour — just a feeling that it was not for me. At present I do a lot of collage work, but may be in the future I will change. No one should stay doing the same thing for too long. ❜

WERNER

❝ *My work is always very varied – I*
can't say I work in one medium, because I use everything, I change
constantly depending on the commission. Unlike other illustrators,
I work exclusively in fashion – but fashion of all kinds. For
instance, I might work for The Wool Fashion Office in Paris,
doing 'tendencies'; or work on commissions for ad agencies,
magazines, newspapers – all kinds.

I prefer quick work, to achieve a spontaneity in the image. I do
not like to spend days or weeks on a project. Fashion interests me
because I like to see how people express their personality in dress,
and to capture the individuality is the point to me.

I work to any scale, depending on the commission. Sometimes
my drawings are ten centimetres, blown up to a metre say for a
poster. You grow used to visualising the finished impact of such a
drawing – after all I have been working in this field for thirty years!

I trained in Hamburg, at a university-type school of
advertising. You did various courses, I learned a lot
about magazine design in my time there and in the last
two years switched to fashion. This solid background
was a great advantage to me. **❞**

TY WILSON

❝ *Perhaps this picture is one of the strongest pieces I have ever done, it is certainly indicative of the way I work. It is essential to get three things: energy, line and colour. I am very concerned with the challenge of fashion illustration, which is to bring down the image to its simplest terms. Simplicity is the thing. I wanted to get the mood and essence of the garment, and in this instance the face was not essential. This applies only in certain situations.*

My approach is a bit like a gas boiler – I can turn it up to high volume or right down to a slow simmer – it depends on the designer. Donna Karan, Azzedine Alaia, Jean-Paul Gaultier, for example, lend themselves to this treatment, concentrating on the drama of the figure.

I work always with a brush. I am influenced by oriental art in my technique. The brush defines the shape, then I apply flat colour, or a pastel, depending on the feeling, for instance to make the big, soft flowers you see in Lacroix. I use flat colour sheets, Pantone; in the past I employed air brush, but I am too impatient for that sometimes.

In the late eighties, shapes are becoming less military, less of the high-shouldered look, but fashion is still very body-conscious. Simplicity is still there, and it is the hardest thing to do. You must remember that it is rooted in the body. You must know the body; only then can you abstract it. With my background in fine art, my concern is not just to draw pretty pictures of pretty clothes, but to consider the shapes they cause on the page. An illustration stands on how it evokes the essence of the garment. I do not think photography and illustration compete against each other. They do different things; what fashion illustration does uniquely is set the mood. ❞

ZOLTAN

❛ *I am Hungarian, and I worked in Budapest for three years, on a fashion magazine and as a freelance photographer for theatres and exhibitions. In 1979 I left Hungary and was given political asylum in Britain. Here I did a fashion and business studies BA course, and began my work as an illustrator in 1981.*

My first commission in England was for Vogue; *they commissioned four pages on Japanese fashion – quite a cultural shock for me at the time. Recently I did some advertising work for Issey Miyake, and I have many other clients in Japan. I work for European magazines, such as* Donna *in Italy,* Vogue, Harper's & Queen *in London, and American* Vogue.

I do fashion, advertising, record covers – a whole range of image-making. Photography still plays a significant part in my work – I like to use various techniques, mixing illustration with photography, where the outcome is never obvious. Distortions, painted or retouched prints, multi-exposed images – all these play their part. Occasionally now I go to video and paintbox-computer images, strictly keeping to the quality of illustration and photography. I also do fashion photography, which I think bothers people who like to keep you in one category.

I have to say it was easier to get work when I first arrived in England than it is now. I am much busier with foreign clients than British ones, and this is sad as I do not want to be one of those refugees who comes here for asylum and then goes away to make a good living somewhere else. But there is much less encouragement for an artist here than in Europe. For example, if one magazine in Italy uses you, then everyone else sees that work and rings up to find out what you could do for them. One Italian magazine tracked me down all the way to London to offer me a regular contract. The only way I keep inspired is by travelling abroad as much as possible. ❜

Zoltan

INDEX

Figures in italics refer to illustrations

ACKNOWLEDGEMENTS

Colin Barnes would like to thank Frances Kennett, Mary Lee Woolf, Veneta Bullen, and the team at Macdonald Orbis for their enthusiastic support. Also to Christopher Alderson for the suit featured in the colour exercise on page 41.
And thanks to Izzie Bricknell, Lucille Lewin and Ben Frankel.

The publishers would like to thank the following for permission to use their photographs:

8, 9, Michael Holford; 10, 11 above Victoria & Albert Museum; 11 below Bildarchiv Preussischer Kulturbesitz; 14 right Archiv für Kunst und Gescichte; 20 right Mary Evans Picture Library; 32 Aldus Archive, © DACS 1988; 33 Fogg Art Museum, Harvard University. Bequest of Meta and Paul F. Sachs; 44, 71, 89 Maison Marie Claire.

Every attempt has been made to trace the copyright owners. Macdonald Orbis therefore offers its apologies to any person or organisation to whom it has failed to give the appropriate acknowledgement.